Egypt of the
Pharaohs

Titles in the World History Series

WORLD
HISTORY SERIES ∎∎∎

Egypt of the Pharaohs

by
Brenda Smith

Lucent Books, P.O. Box 289011, San Diego, CA 92198-9011

Library of Congress Cataloging-in-Publication Data

Smith, Brenda, 1946-
   Egypt of the pharaohs / by Brenda Smith.
      p. cm.—(World history series)
   Includes bibliographical references and index.
Summary: Discusses the dynasties of the Egyptian pharaohs
and the impact of their rule on their own country and the
ancient world.
   ISBN 1-56006-241-X   (alk. paper)
   1. Egypt—History—To 332 B.C.—Juvenile literature.
[1. Egypt—History—To 332 B.C.]   I. Title. II. Series.
DT83.S63   1996
932—dc20   95-36664
                                             CIP
                                             AC

Copyright 1996 by Lucent Books, Inc., P.O. Box 289011,
San Diego, California, 92198-9011

Printed in the U.S.A.

Acknowledgments

Many thanks to my friends and colleagues, Robert A. Kohan and Victoria Cox Kaser, for their invaluable assistance in reviewing the manuscript, and to my husband, Duane, for his unfailing patience, encouragement, and love.

Contents

Foreword

Each year on the first day of school, nearly every history teacher faces the task of explaining why his or her students should study history. One logical answer to this question is that exploring what happened in our past explains how the things we often take for granted—our customs, ideas, and institutions—came to be. As statesman and historian Winston Churchill put it, "Every nation or group of nations has its own tale to tell. Knowledge of the trials and struggles is necessary to all who would comprehend the problems, perils, challenges, and opportunities which confront us today." Thus, a study of history puts modern ideas and institutions in perspective. For example, though the founders of the United States were talented and creative thinkers, they clearly did not invent the concept of democracy. Instead, they adapted some democratic ideas that had originated in ancient Greece and with which the Romans, the British, and others had experimented. An exploration of these cultures, then, reveals their very real connection to us through institutions that continue to shape our daily lives.

Another reason often given for studying history is the idea that lessons exist in the past from which contemporary societies can benefit and learn. This idea, although controversial, has always been an intriguing one for historians. Those that agree that society can benefit from the past often quote philosopher George Santayana's famous statement, "Those who cannot remember the past are condemned to repeat it." Historians who ascribe to Santayana's philosophy believe that, for example, studying the events that led up to the major world wars or other significant historical events would allow society to chart a different and more favorable course in the future.

Just as difficult as convincing students to realize the importance of studying history is the search for useful and interesting supplementary materials that present historical events in a context that can be easily understood. The volumes in Lucent Books' World History Series attempt to present a broad, balanced, and penetrating view of the march of history. Ancient Egypt's important wars and rulers, for example, are presented against the rich and colorful backdrop of Egyptian religious, social, and cultural developments. The series engages the reader by enhancing historical events with these cultural contexts. For example, in *Ancient Greece*, the text covers the role of women in that society. Slavery is discussed in *The Roman Empire*, as well as how slaves earned their freedom. The numerous and varied aspects of everyday life in these and other societies are explored in each volume of the series. Additionally, the series covers the major political, cultural, and philosophical ideas as the torch of civilization is passed from ancient Mesopotamia and Egypt, through Greece, Rome, Medieval Europe, and other world cultures, to the modern day.

The material in the series is formatted in a thorough, precise, and organized manner. Each volume offers the reader a comprehensive and clearly written overview of an important historical event or period. The topic under discussion is placed in a broad historical context. For example, *The Italian Renaissance* begins with a discussion of the High Middle Ages and the loss of central control that allowed certain Italian cities to develop artistically. The book ends by looking forward to the Reformation and interpreting the societal changes that grew out of the Renaissance. Thus, students are not only involved in an historical era, but also enveloped by the events leading up to that era and the events following it.

One important and unique feature in the World History Series is the primary and secondary source quotations that richly supplement each volume. These quotes are useful in a number of ways. First, they allow students access to sources they would not normally be exposed to because of the difficulty and obscurity of the original source. The quotations range from interesting anecdotes to farsighted cultural perspectives and are drawn from historical witnesses both past and present. Second, the quotes demonstrate how and where historians themselves derive their information on the past as they strive to reach a consensus on historical events. Lastly, all of the quotes are footnoted, familiarizing students with the citation process and allowing them to verify quotes and/or look up the original source if the quote piques their interest.

Finally, the books in the World History Series provide a detailed launching point for further research. Each book contains a bibliography specifically geared toward student research. A second, annotated bibliography introduces students to all the sources the author consulted when compiling the book. A chronology of important dates gives students an overview, at a glance, of the topic covered. Where applicable, a glossary of terms is included.

In short, the series is designed not only to acquaint readers with the basics of history, but also to make them aware that their lives are a part of an ongoing human saga. Perhaps they will then come to the same realization as famed historian Arnold Toynbee. In his monumental work, *A Study of History*, he wrote about becoming aware of history flowing through him in a mighty current, and of his own life "welling like a wave in the flow of this vast tide."

Important Dates in the History of Egypt of the Pharaohs

B.C. 5500	5000	4500	4000	3500	3000

B.C.

5500
Predynastic Period begins; agriculture begins

4000
Egyptians develop a writing system, called hieroglyphics, and a calendar

3100
Early Dynastic Period begins; Menes unites Upper and Lower Egypt and becomes its first pharaoh; Memphis becomes first capital

2700
Old Kingdom begins; Re becomes chief god

2639
Architect Imhotep builds first pyramid for pharaoh Djoser

2560
Khufu builds the Great Pyramid at Giza

2200
First Intermediate Period; Egypt experiences political upheaval; famine leads to widespread revolts throughout Egypt; nobles and priests become more powerful than pharaoh; Egypt splits into independent regions

2160
Nomarchs from the district of Herakleopolis seize throne

2040
Middle Kingdom begins; Theban Mentuhotep II reunites Egypt; Amen and Osiris become nationally important gods

1991
Capital moved to Itj-tawy, near Memphis; Golden Age in art and literature begins; Egypt conquers Nubia, a land to its south; temple to Amen-Re built at Karnak

1674
Second Intermediate Period begins when foreigners called Hyksos conquer Egypt; Hyksos conquerors introduce horse and chariot

1552
Ahmose drives Hyksos out of Egypt and reunifies the country; New Kingdom begins; Amen-Re becomes national god; pharaohs move away from pyramid burials and begin building cliff tombs in the Valley of the Kings

2500	2000	1500	1000	500	A.D. 500	640

1478
Hatshepsut seizes throne and rules as the first female pharaoh

1458
Thutmose III regains throne

1456
Thutmose III wins Battle of Megiddo

1352
Pharaoh Akhenaten proclaims a new god, Aten, for Egypt, and loses lands Egyptians had conquered

1336
Tutankhamen restores Amen-Re

1294
Seti I begins reconquest of lands lost by Akhenaten

1279
Ramses II (the Great) ascends throne to begin sixty-seven-year rule

1275
Ramses II is victorious at Kadesh

1178
Ramses III fights off Sea Peoples

1069
Egypt once more splits into two lands—Upper and Lower Egypt

945
Libyans seize throne

720
Kushite Piankhy becomes pharaoh

670
Assyrians conquer Egypt

663
Saite 26th Dynasty restores some of Egypt's greatness

525
Egypt becomes part of Persian Empire

343
Last native-born Egyptian pharaoh, Nectanebo II, loses throne

332
The Greeks, under Alexander the Great, conquer Egypt

30
Egypt becomes a Roman province

A.D.

640
Arabs and Islam conquer Egypt

Ancient Clues

In the fall of 1922, British archaeologist Howard Carter had been excavating sites in Egypt's Valley of the Kings for six years. Tirelessly he had searched for the tombs of ancient Egypt's last great pharaohs, or kings, who had been laid to rest more than three thousand years before. Carter wanted to find one tomb—just one—that had not been robbed of the treasures that had been buried with these rulers. Time and time again, he had been disappointed. Today, November 4, was different, and Carter was almost dizzy with excitement. As he was preparing to open a sealed door to a tomb, he felt he was about to make the discovery of a lifetime. If he was right, this was the tomb of Tutankhamen, the boy-king who ruled Egypt from 1336 to 1327 B.C.

Carter's hands were trembling as he began to make a tiny hole in the door. Carefully he widened it until there was room to insert a candle. Lord Carnarvon, who had financed the expedition, and two other friends anxiously awaited the archaeologist's verdict. Carter later described what he saw:

> At first I could see nothing, the hot air escaping from the chamber causing the candle flames to flicker, but presently, as my eyes grew accustomed

In a quest to uncover some of the mysteries of ancient Egypt, Howard Carter (left) and an assistant stand in the doorway to the tomb of Tutankhamen, one of Egypt's most well-known pharaohs.

to the light, details of the room within emerged slowly from the mist, strange animals, statues, and gold—everywhere the glint of gold. For the moment—an eternity it must have seemed to the others standing by—I was struck dumb with amazement, and when Lord Carnarvon, unable to stand the suspense any longer, inquired anxiously, "Can you see anything?" it was all I could do to get out the words, "Yes, wonderful things!"[1]

After widening the opening, Carter and the others ventured into the tomb.

Everything was exactly as it had been more than three thousand years before, when the pharaoh was buried. In addition to a glorious gilt throne, there were beds, couches, chairs, chariots, stone jars containing food, chests filled with linen clothing, and a beautiful ostrich-feather fan in perfect condition. There was even the scent of perfume that had lingered through the centuries. In another chamber lay a huge gilt shrine. Inside were three nested coffins, the innermost of which was made of solid gold and held the mummy of the pharaoh, perfectly preserved.

Carter examines the solid gold coffin that holds the mummy of the young pharaoh Tutankhamen. By studying the remains of ancient Egypt, archaeologists such as Carter learn valuable information about the lives of Egyptian pharaohs.

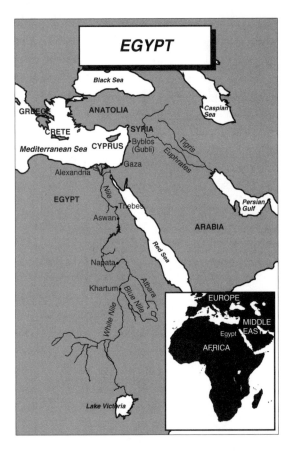

EGYPT

When the lid of the last coffin was removed, Carter stood gazing at a gleaming golden mask bearing the image of Tutankhamen. Lying on it was a wreath of flowers that had probably been placed there by Ankhesenamen, the pharaoh's young widow. Carter was so moved that he later wrote:

> Among all that regal splendour, that royal magnificence . . . there was nothing so beautiful as those few withered flowers. . . . They told us what a short period 3,300 years really was.[2]

For the next ten years, Carter and other archaeologists studied the remains of ancient Egyptian society found in Tutankhamen's tomb. In this way, they provided people in modern times with information about life in the land of the pharaohs. Carter's discovery was particularly important because Tutankhamen's tomb was the only royal resting place that had not been violated by robbers, who often destroyed ancient evidence.

An Enduring Civilization

Based on information gathered from Tutankhamen's tomb and other sites in Egypt, archaeologists believe that ancient Egypt produced the first and most enduring civilization of all time. It began about five thousand years ago in the fertile Nile River Valley of northeastern Africa. Over time the Egyptians became supremely confident in their institutions and way of life, which was centered around an all-powerful, divine pharaoh. The prosperity and strength of the Egyptian state was tied directly to the fortunes of its ruler. When the pharaohs were strong, Egypt experienced times of growth and glory. But if the ruler's control weakened, the country went through periods of chaos and bloodshed.

Even during troubled times, however, Egypt's civilization remained largely intact. Other ancient societies, especially those of Greece and Rome, marveled at its achievements. Through the Greeks and Romans, the achievements of the Egyptians in astronomy, mathematics, architecture, medicine, writing, and literature have been passed down and have influenced Western civilization. These accomplishments, along with precious treasures, remain to testify to the greatness of this ancient land.

1 The Roots of Egyptian Civilization

More than any other factor, the geography of Egypt, especially the mighty Nile River, shaped Egyptian civilization. As virtually the only source of water, the Nile sustained all life in Egypt, a fertile, green area that resembled a giant flower surrounded by desert. The 750-mile-long narrow strip of river and fertile soil of the Nile Valley made up the stem of the flower. The flower's blossom was the triangular, marshy plain called the Delta, where the Nile's waters empty into the Mediterranean Sea. Egyptologist James Henry Breasted commented that the change from fertile, river-fed land to barren desert sands was so abrupt that a person could stand with one foot in each.

The Gift of the Nile

Each spring, heavy rains and melting snows at the source of the Nile in the mountains of central Africa sent tons of water rushing down the river. From July to October, the Nile spilled over its banks and spread its life-giving waters over the thirsty land. As the floodwaters receded, they left behind a layer of fertile, black mud. The ancient Egyptians held a deep reverence for the Nile, recognizing, as the

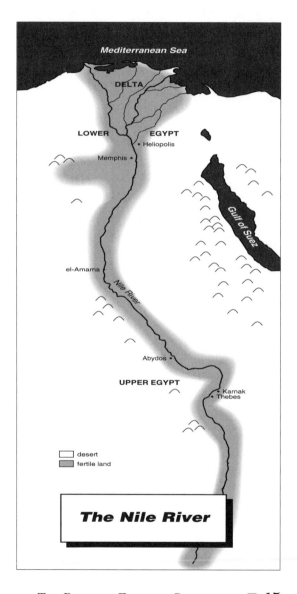

The Nile River

Shining Like Pale Silver

Many historians argue that a people's character is formed in part by their environment. The Egyptians were no exception. In Life Under the Pharaohs, *author Leonard Cottrell describes ancient Egypt through the eyes of an imaginary sky god.*

"I imagine some watcher from the skies, a sky deity, looking down on this green serpent, the Nile Valley, coiling through the desert waste for 600 miles . . . never more than a few miles wide and often less than a mile in width. On the west stretches an endless waste of sand and rock—the Sahara. On the other side the Arabian Desert rolls eastward for hundreds of miles until it reaches the Red Sea. There is a full moon and my sky-god would see the great river shining like pale silver. Here and there he would see a sprinkling of lights along the banks. . . . But he would not see the hundreds of unlighted villages where millions of fellahin [present-day Egyptian peasants] sleep the sleep of exhaustion, huddled in their mud-brick villages, until the sun calls them out to the flat fields to continue their eternal labors. To how many millions of souls has this green snake given birth during the past hundred centuries? As an immortal, my sky-god would remember the time when the green gash in the desert was known only to animals, birds, and reptiles; when lions and hyenas, cheetahs and wolves roamed the desert fringes, and hippopotami splashed in the water; when huge flocks of geese rose above the papyrus marshes in clouds, before man was known in the valley.

My god would have seen how century after century, the jungle gave way to cultivation. He would have seen, for the first time on this planet, ordered cities developing, surrounded by fields, threaded by roads and canals, while the rest of the human race, or most of it, still wandered from hunting ground to hunting ground."

Greek historian Herodotus said, that Egypt itself was "the gift of the Nile."[3] An ancient hymn reflects this feeling:

Hail O Nile, who issues forth from the earth, who comes to give life to the people of Egypt. Secret of movement, a darkness in daylight. Praised by his followers whose fields you water. Created by Re [sun god] to give life to all who thirst. Who lets the desert drink with streams descending from heaven.

Beloved of the earth-god, controller of the corn god, who causes the workshops of Ptah [god of artists and craftsworkers] to flourish. Lord of fish who causes the water-fowl to sail upstream . . . who makes barley and creates wheat so the temples celebrate. . . . When the Nile overflows, offerings are made to you, cattle are slaughtered for you, a great oblation [offering] is made to you, birds are fattened for you, desert lions are trapped for you that your goodness be repaid.[4]

Ancient Egyptians depended on the annual flooding of the Nile to sustain their agricultural lifestyle. Egyptians planted wheat, barley, and corn seeds in the wet soil. Farming yields fed both the people and the livestock they raised. The Egyptians settled in permanent villages, building sturdy, one-story houses of bricks made from Nile mud and a little straw.

In addition to providing a source of food, the Nile protected the growing Egyptian civilization. To the east and west, beyond the river's reach, lay the desert wastelands, stretching as far as the eye could see. To the north was the Delta, whose marshy coastline offered no harbor to ships. To the south were a series of churning, boulder-filled rapids called cataracts, which made travel down the Nile into Egypt difficult for boats. Although nomadic desert dwellers sometimes raided Egyptian villages, the country's natural boundaries, created in part by the Nile, kept potential conquerors at bay for centuries. As a result, the Egyptians suffered few enemy invasions and could devote themselves to developing their civilization.

Besides helping to keep enemies out, the Nile provided a unique link between villages. The long, narrow Nile Valley, known as Upper Egypt, was in many places only twelve miles wide. Villages were strung out over an unusually long area running from north to south. In the Delta, or Lower Egypt, villages were scattered along seven different branches of the Nile.

Although the gigantic boulders of the cataracts kept foreign enemies from using the river to attack from the south, within Egypt the Nile was very navigable, making transportation and communication between settlements easy. The river served as a broad highway enabling the pharaohs to unite Egypt politically and a common civilization to develop.

Using Their Wits

Although the Nile itself was predictable, its flood levels varied from year to year. Thousands would starve to death if floodwaters were too high and destroyed homes, stored grain, and seeds for the next year's planting. If floodwaters were too low, they enriched fewer acres, and less food crops could be planted and harvested. In such years, too, thousands starved to death. As Egyptologist Adolf Erman observed, "The days of inundation [flooding] were . . . days of anxiety and care."[5]

Between 5500 and 3100 B.C., during the Predynastic Period—the time before the Delta and the Nile Valley were united under the first dynasty, or family, of pharaohs—the Egyptians created an intricate irrigation system. They dug basins in the earth that served as reservoirs to trap the floodwaters. Then they dug canals to carry the water from these basins to fields farther from the river—fields that even high floodwaters might not reach. The Egyptians also built dikes, or earthen banks, to reinforce the basins' walls.

Egypt's irrigation system needed constant maintenance to mend damaged basins and canals. In time the Egyptians made further improvements, including the use of a shadoof, a device with a bucket attached to a pole that lifted water from the Nile into the canals and from the canals into the fields. Egyptian irrigation systems were so successful that farmers could grow not one but two or three crops in a season.

One ancient Egyptian source described the land at this time:

> [Egypt's] channels abound in fish and its lakes in birds. Its fields are green with herbage [greenery] and its banks bear dates. Its . . . granaries [storehouses for grain] are overflowing with barley and wheat. Garlic, wheat, lettuces, and fruits are there for sustenance [supporting life and health] and wine surpassing honey. He who dwells there is happy for there the humble are like the mighty elsewhere.[6]

Changes in Society

Farming brought dramatic changes to Egyptian society. The abundance of food allowed individuals freedom from constant food gathering and time for specialization, or the development of occupations. So while most Egyptians still worked in the fields, some became, for example, potters, making decorative clay bowls and jars. Weavers spun thread from flax, another Egyptian crop, and wove it into linen clothing. Stone carvers ground and polished stone into statues, knives, and ax heads. Metalworkers hammered copper into

Detail from a thirteenth-century B.C. wall painting depicts an Egyptian using a shadoof, an irrigation device used by farmers to draw water from the Nile.

The fertile Nile Valley supplied an abundance of food, making agriculture an important industry in Egypt. A relief depicts Egyptian agricultural scenes including harvesting crops and herding cattle.

weapons and tools. Some even may have melted copper to use in molds, an innovation that probably made its way to Egypt via immigrants who trickled into the northern corners of the Delta from the Near East. Together these early artisans, or skilled craftsworkers, formed the beginning of a new social class, distinct from the majority of villagers, who were peasants and still worked the land.

Specialization led to trade, which changed Egypt's economy and helped the country grow. The various craftsworkers no longer had a direct connection to the land and needed a way to get food for themselves. So they traded the goods they made for agricultural workers' produce. Soon, trade extended beyond individual villages to neighboring settlements along the Nile. Before long, a class of merchants, people who bought and sold goods, developed. They took their place in the developing class structure alongside the artisans. Using a barter system, as the Egyptians had no money, these merchants ferried goods in canoes or sometimes transported them overland in donkey caravans. As one ancient Egyptian source said, "The merchants sail upstream and downstream, busy as bees."[7]

Mice in the Fields

Agriculture was the Egyptians' most important industry, but the peasants who farmed the land led no easy life. A letter by an unknown author describing all the hardships faced by the peasant is quoted in Adolf Erman's Life in Ancient Egypt.

"The worm has taken half of the food, the hippopotamus the other half; there were mice in the fields, the locusts have come down, and the cattle have eaten, and the sparrows have stolen. Poor miserable agriculturalist! What was left on the threshing floor, thieves made away with. . . . Then the scribe lands on the [river] bank to receive the harvest [taxes for the pharaoh]; his followers carry sticks. . . . They say, 'Give up the corn'—there is none there. Then they beat him [the farmer] as he lies stretched out and bound on the ground. They throw him into the canal and he sinks down, head under water. His wife is bound before his eyes and his children are put in fetters."

Farming in ancient Egypt was a difficult lifework. In addition to hard labor in the fields, farmers faced animal predators and brutal tax collectors.

The Growth of Government

Agriculture brought one final, critical change—the growth of government in ancient Egypt. More sophisticated farming made society more complicated. The irrigation system had to be built and maintained. After the annual floods, land had to be divided for planting. Grain surpluses had to be stored and, in times of need, distributed. Trade had to be conducted. Quarrels over land ownership had to be settled. Gradually, a government to plan and direct these activities developed from the existing tribal structure.

Most Egyptians belonged to a tribe, and every village belonged to one of a number of independent tribal territories, or districts. Each was governed by a chief to whom all the villagers in the district owed their loyalty. The chief ruled from the capital city of the district, which was usually his home village.

Along with the tribal districts, a few city-states existed in predynastic Egypt. Each consisted of a town or a city and the countryside around it and was ruled by a king who wielded the same level of authority as a district chief. Like the districts, each city-state had its own market, local god, temple, and totem (symbol) of the ruler's clan, or extended family. Generally, city-states developed when one town became more prosperous or powerful than others, and its leaders extended their authority over neighboring villages.

Stronger states continued to conquer or absorb weaker ones, through war and sometimes marriage, until eventually Egypt was made up of just two kingdoms. Lower Egypt, which encompassed the Nile's Delta region, had its capital at Buto in the western Delta. Nekheb, located at the site of present-day el-Kab, served as the capital of Upper Egypt, which at this time included all the land in the Nile Valley stretching from the Delta to the Nile's first cataract near Aswan in southern Egypt. For hundreds of years, these two kingdoms existed side by side. Their unification would propel ancient Egypt into its greatest age.

2 The Old Kingdom: Egypt's Greatest Age

Around 3100 B.C., six hundred years before what is called the Old Kingdom began, a king of Upper Egypt named Menes conquered Lower Egypt and united the country. With unification, Egypt became the first nation in world history, and Menes became its first king, later called pharaoh. Guided by Menes and the pharaohs who succeeded him, Egyptian civilization grew increasingly more advanced, organized, and prosperous during the following six centuries. A paper made from papyrus reeds was invented, a kind of picture writing called hieroglyphics was devised, and taxes were levied. The stage was set for the beginning of an era known as the Old Kingdom. During the Old Kingdom—Egypt's greatest age—pharaohs were the nation's all-powerful rulers. Religion, art, trade, architecture, literature—even social and economic life—were all established and cultivated by the pharaohs to reinforce their centralized authority.

A carved palette found in Upper Egypt preserves the likeness of King Narmer, thought to be another name for Menes, Egypt's first king.

All-Powerful Kings

The pharaohs of Egypt were autocrats, or rulers with absolute power. Their word was law and was obeyed unconditionally.

The pharaohs controlled the nation not only politically, but also spiritually. Although it is unclear how the people came to view their pharaoh as a god, what is known is that by the Old Kingdom the pharaoh was considered to be the son of Re, the Egyptian sun god.

At his approach, the ruler's subjects showed their reverence by flinging themselves face down and touching their heads to the ground. One ancient Egyptian source described the pharaoh's power and wisdom:

> What is there that thou dost not know? Who is there that is as wise as thou? What place is there which thou hast not seen? . . . Every circumstance hath come to thine ears since thou hast administered this land. . . . If thou sayest to the waters, "Come upon the mountain," a flood floweth directly at thy word, for thou art Re. . . . Authority is in thy mouth and perception is in thy heart; the activity of thy tongue is the temple of Maat [the goddess of truth], and God sitteth upon thy lips. . . . Thou art destined for eternity. All is done according to thy will, and whatever thou sayest is obeyed.[8]

As both the king and the son of Re, the pharaoh was the center of Egyptian life. He and the royal family were at the top of Egypt's social pyramid, followed by the priests, high officials, and nobles. Scribes, skilled artisans of all kinds, and petty officials were next, followed by the largest class, the common laborers and peasant-farmers.

The pharaoh acted as a strong, unifying political force; Egypt's prosperity was believed to be directly due to the influence of the pharaoh, who interceded with other gods to bring blessings to the land.

Though a few Egyptian nobles owned property privately, in fact the pharaoh owned most of the land in Egypt, acquired through conquest and inheritance. The pharaoh parceled out some estates to a few favored nobles—descendants of former kings and landed nobility from earlier times—to control for their lifetimes.

In addition, the pharaoh owned most everything produced on the land. Because the Egyptians did not have a system of money, taxes were collected in the form of wheat, barley, olive oil, beer, wine, and fruit. The pharaoh then used these revenues to pay out wages for royal officials, craftsworkers, priests, and other laborers.

By the time of the Old Kingdom, Egyptians revered the pharaoh as the son of the hawk-headed Egyptian sun god Re (pictured).

All the work on the land was done by peasants, who made up the bulk of the population. Though not exactly slaves, peasants in ancient Egypt were similar to serfs in medieval Europe because they were tied to the land. If the land changed hands for any reason, they went with it. Also like serfs, peasants were allowed to work small plots for their own subsistence crops only when they were finished with their tasks in the landlord's fields.

To help maintain this absolute power while conducting the daily business of Egypt, the Old Kingdom pharaohs created a new, highly centralized system of government that would remain in place throughout ancient Egyptian history. A central government was established at Memphis— a city near the junction of Upper Egypt and Lower Egypt—to direct the local activities of the various provinces, later called nomes. At first, all high-ranking positions were held by the pharaoh's relatives, but eventually, commoners were appointed to some of the highest offices of government.

The pharaoh, of course, was at the top of this hierarchy. The next most powerful position was the office of vizier, whose staggering duties included oversight of many of the central government's departments, which were staffed with a huge number of officials, called scribes. The vizier made sure that taxes were collected, fields were cultivated, and the irrigation system was maintained. He was also responsible for administering the judicial system across the land, and as if that were not enough, he often acted as the king's chief architect.

On the local level, the borders of Egypt's nomes generally conformed to ancient tribal districts. There were twenty-two local governments in Upper Egypt and, eventually, twenty in Lower Egypt.

Each was a miniature state with departments corresponding to those of the central government. Each nome had a governor, called a nomarch, who was appointed by the pharaoh. The nomarch reported to the vizier and, like the vizier, had diverse duties. He served as chief judge of the province, supervised irrigation, stored grain for emergencies, and collected taxes on the pharaoh's estates in his province. The governor also sent soldiers from his nome's militia—usually untrained peasants—to fight for the pharaoh in emergencies because Egypt as yet had no national army.

Many Gods and Goddesses

Religion was vital to the ancient Egyptians. In addition to deifying their pharaoh, they recognized and worshiped as many as two thousand other gods. Even some two thousand years later, when Greek historian Herodotus visited the land of the pharaohs, he observed, "There seem to be more gods than men in Egypt."[9]

The Egyptians believed that gods governed nature and every aspect of life, from birth to death. Some gods took on human form, others were in animal form, and others were a combination, with human bodies and animal heads. The origins of these gods have been only partially identified. Some originated in the Predynastic Period, when each village, city, and province claimed specific gods. In time, some became more widely recognized and became the great gods and goddesses of the Egyptian nation.

The most important god during the Old Kingdom was the hawk-headed sun

As Bitter as Gall

As the highest official in the state, the vizier had great responsibilities. Each time a new vizier was installed, the reigning pharaoh gave a speech about the vizier's duties, which is quoted in When Egypt Ruled the East *by George Steindorff and Keith C. Seele.*

"As to the office of vizier . . . it is not pleasant; no, it is as bitter as gall. . . . He is one who must give no special consideration to princes or councilors nor win to himself anyone as a follower. . . . Now if a petitioner [person with a request] comes from Upper or Lower Egypt . . . then you must . . . see to it that everything is done according to law and . . . is conducted in a proper manner, while every man is accorded his rights. . . . Look upon him whom you know as on him whom you do not know, the one who is close to you as the one who is distant from you. . . . Pass over no petitioner without hearing his case. . . . Show anger to no man wrongfully and be angry only at that which deserves anger. Instill fear of yourself [make people fear you] . . . for a true official is an official who is feared. . . . But if a man instills fear in an excessive manner [too much] . . . then they do not say of him: 'That is a just man. . . .' What one expects of the conduct of the vizier is the performance of justice; for it is the vizier who has been its proper keeper since [the rule of] the god."

god, Re. Egyptians believed he was born each morning in the east, sailed across the heavens during the day, and died as an old man in the west each night. During the night, he traveled through the Underworld, the region where the dead resided, to reach the east again. One ancient Egyptian source described Re as "exalted over the vault of the sky, bringing the sun to life every day."[10]

Joining Re among the great gods was Osiris, lord of the dead, who ruled the Underworld. The Egyptians believed that Osiris once ruled Egypt. In fact, he was depicted as a mummified pharaoh wearing a crown and carrying other symbols of his office. While on the throne, Osiris was murdered by his brother Seth, the god of storms and violence, who was usually pictured with a man's body and the head of a fierce but unknown beast. However, Osiris's death, according to Egyptian myth, was avenged by his son Horus, often represented as a hawk. The other major gods included Anubis, Thoth, and Hathor. Anubis, the god of embalming, had the head of a jackal, an animal that often prowled around cemeteries. Thoth,

A painted wood sculpture of the Egyptian god Osiris, ruler of the Underworld. Egyptians believed that the worthy would join Osiris in the Underworld after death.

depicted with the head of an ibis—an Egyptian bird—, was the god of writing and wisdom. And the cow-headed goddess, Hathor, protected women.

The pharaoh was the chief priest of all Egypt. In theory, he provided for the gods and cared for their images, which were kept in a temple's innermost sanctuary, called the holy of holies. In return, the gods inhabited their images and showered their blessings on the pharaoh and Egypt. In practice, however, the priests, acting as representatives of the pharaoh, performed the required rituals.

The pharaoh built huge temples dedicated to the gods throughout the land. However, an Egyptian temple was not like a modern-day church, mosque, or synagogue where people gather to worship. Rather, it was considered the god's home, and only the pharaoh and the priests were allowed to enter. The people participated in the worship of the state gods only on special festival days. Yet they were deeply religious, worshiping local gods at smaller shrines in their area and household gods at altars in their homes. In fact, Herodotus reported, "The Egyptians are religious . . . beyond any other nation in the world."[11]

The Dead Live Again

A fundamental part of Egyptian religion was the belief in an afterlife. Several explanations were common. In one, the dead inhabited a field in the heavens called the "field of Yaru." In this place, not unlike agricultural Egypt, the dead lived in peace and plenty. Some people unable to reach Yaru, which was surrounded by water,

Murder Most Foul

The ancient Egyptians had many myths that explained the origin of the world. Out of them, their great gods developed. One of the greatest gods was Osiris, who suffered a dire fate at the hands of his brother Seth. Author Leonard Cottrell tells the story in Life Under the Pharaohs.

"Osiris succeeded to the throne of his father and governed the world wisely and justly, aided by his sister Isis, whom he married. Seth, jealous of his brother's power, plotted to destroy him and eventually succeeded, afterwards cutting the body of Osiris into pieces which he buried in several parts of Egypt. The head was buried at Abydos. The faithful Isis recovered the scattered fragments of her husband's corpse, and with the aid of the jackal-god Anubis, who subsequently became the god of embalmment, re-animated it. Though unable to return to his life on earth, Osiris passed to the Underworld, where he became the god of the dead and later the judge of souls. Isis bore a son, Horus, who afterwards took revenge on his uncle Seth, defeating the usurper [the man who had seized the throne by force] in battle and winning back his father's throne."

Osiris (pictured) became the god of the Underworld and judge of souls after he was murdered by his jealous brother Seth. Egyptians believed that worshiping Osiris ensured eternal life after death.

The jackal-god Anubis sits atop a shrine found in the tomb of Tutankhamen. Anubis was the god of the dead and of embalming.

enlisted the aid of sacred animals. Egyptologist James Henry Breasted describes the journey:

> Sometimes the departed might induce the hawk or the ibis to bear him across. . . . Sometimes the sun god bore him across on his barque [boat]. But by far the majority depended upon the services of a ferryman called "Turn-face" or "Look-behind," because his face was ever turned to the rear in poling his craft. He will not receive all into his boat, but only him of whom it was said, "there is no evil which he has done."[12]

According to many historians, this was the first time in history that people believed the quality of life after death depended on the actions and behaviors of the living.

Later, the Egyptians came to believe that the worthy dead went beneath Egypt to the Underworld to join Osiris, and that only the all-powerful pharaoh and his family, along with a few nobles and high officials, were entitled to enter the afterlife. Even those in the ruler's immediate circle, however, could not get to the Underworld unless he actually led them. So, to be near his spirit, the nobles built their tombs as close to his as possible, with land and materials often provided by the pharaoh. Ordinary Egyptians, who could not enter the afterlife, continued to bury their dead in shallow pits in the sand beyond the tombs of the pharaoh and the nobles.

The Pharaoh's Journey

The ancient Egyptians believed the pharaoh's soul required a body in order to make the journey to the afterlife. Furthermore, if that body were allowed to decay after death, the spirit, or *ka*, would be condemned to wander alone for all eternity. The Egyptians wanted to ensure their ruler's successful trip to the next world, where they believed he would ensure the safety of his people for eternity. So, they developed a special process, called mummification, that preserved the dead pharaoh's body, as well as the bodies of family members and selected nobles who would be allowed entrance into the Underworld.

When a pharaoh died, servants carried his body to a temple near his tomb. First, the priest-embalmers gently laid their ruler on a narrow table and removed his internal organs to keep them from rotting. Then, they inserted a long hook into the nostrils and pulled out the brain piece by piece. The only organ they did not remove was the heart, for it was considered the center of the soul.

After the organs were removed, the body was washed with palm wine, filled with incense and perfumes, and stitched closed again. The embalmers then covered it with natron, a special kind of salt, to dry up the fluid in the body tissues. After seventy days, they washed the now-dried-up body in the Nile and rubbed resins and oils into the skin. Then they wrapped it in strips of fine linen. If all this was performed correctly, Egyptians believed, the dead pharaoh would soon come to life again. According to one ancient source, "Your flesh shall rise up for you, your bones shall fuse themselves for you, your members [body parts] shall collect themselves for you, your flesh shall reassemble for you."[13]

Once the body was mummified, it was time for the funeral. The body was encased within three progressively larger coffins. Then all three were enclosed in an even larger coffin called a sarcophagus and placed on a bier, or coffin stand, which was hauled to the tomb. The priests walked at the head of a long procession, swinging incense and chanting prayers. Behind the priests walked the pharaoh's family, with the weeping queen leading them. She smeared dirt on her face and tore open her dress to show her grief. Last came a long line of mourners, including relatives and court officials. Servants carried furniture, clothing, food, weapons, jewelry, and other items for their dead lord to use in the afterlife.

After the pharaoh was placed in the tomb, the priest performed one final ceremony, which ended with the words, "You will live again, you revive always, you have

Ancient Egyptians believed a dead person's heart would be weighed by the gods to determine the person's worthiness for the afterlife. This papyrus painting portrays Egyptian gods and the scale used to weigh the heart.

The mummified remains of an adult and a child. Thousands of years old, they illustrate the effectiveness of the Egyptian embalming process.

become young again, you are young again, and forever."[14] To nourish the pharaoh's spirit after death, specially appointed priests carried out rituals at his separate mortuary, or funeral, temple.

The Age of Pyramids

The tombs of the great pharaohs were gigantic pyramids—huge stone mountains designed to protect the pharaoh's body forever—clustered at Giza, outside the ancient city of Memphis west of the Nile River. These pyramids were not only tombs, but also symbols of the pharaoh's tremendous power in the here and now. The very process of building them showed how efficiently the ruler could organize the state's resources. The pharaohs of the Old Kingdom built so many pyramids that this time period has been called the Age of Pyramids.

During the Old Kingdom, the pharaoh's chief architect was charged with drawing up plans for the ruler's tomb. One of his first tasks was to make certain that the entrance of the tomb faced due north, which was the custom in ancient Egypt. To do this he drew on the Egyptians' knowledge of astronomy. Workers first built a circular, mud-brick wall to create an artificial horizon. At night, while standing in the circle's center, the architect had an assistant mark the place where a star rose in the sky. When dawn came, the assistant then marked the place where the star set. The men drew a straight line from these two points to the center of the circle and divided in two the angle formed by the lines. The dividing line pointed to true north.

The Egyptians developed mathematics, as well, to help them with their pyramid building. Before undertaking such an enormous task, they had to calculate how much stone was needed, at what exact angle to construct the walls, and what quantity of food the pharaoh had to provide to feed workers. So they invented a system of written numbers based on ten, something like our decimal system. They also developed fractions, using them along with whole numbers to simplify counting, adding, and subtracting. The Egyptians also derived formulas to measure the areas of squares, triangles, and circles as well as the volume of cylinders, spheres, and pyramids.

One junior scribe who had trouble with his figures was sharply scolded by his superior:

For see, thou art the clever scribe. . . . A ramp is to be constructed, 730 cubits [1095 feet] long, 55 cubits [82.5 feet] wide, containing 120 compartments, and filled with reeds and beams; 60 cubits [90 feet] high at its summit, 30 cubits [45 feet] in the middle, with a . . . of 15 cubits [22.5 feet], and its . . . 5 cubits [7.5 feet]. The quantity of the bricks needed for it is

Erecting the pyramids may have looked something like this. The Egyptians developed mathematics to help them determine at what angle to construct the walls and to calculate the quantity of stone needed to complete such a formidable task.

asked of the generals and the scribes . . . without one of them knowing anything. They all put their trust in thee and say: "Thou art a clever scribe, my friend! Decide for us quickly! Behold thy name is famous. . . . Do not let it be said that there is aught [anything] thou dost not know. Answer us, how many bricks are needed for it?"[15]

The tombs of the earliest pharaohs had all been large, single-story rectangular mud-brick slabs called mastabas. The first pyramid was built for Djoser, the first influential pharaoh of the Old Kingdom and founder of the 3rd Dynasty. Unlike modern architects, his chief architect, Imhotep, designed the tomb and supervised its construction without blueprints. To build a tomb that would last, Imhotep decided to use stone instead of mud brick. He began by building a single square mastaba, then topped it with progressively smaller levels until he had constructed the great Step Pyramid, named for its series of giant tiers, or steps. It rose to a height of nearly two hundred feet and was the first large structure of stone in the world.

To My Dear, Dead Wife

In ancient Egypt, people believed that a person who had died could cause grief to the living. In this ancient letter quoted in Leonard Cottrell's Life Under the Pharaohs, *a recent widower, struck down with disease, wrote to his dead wife to lessen her anger.*

"What evil have I done to you, that I should find myself in this wretched state? What then have I done to you, that you should lay your hand upon me, when no evil was done to you? You became my wife when I was young, and I was with you. I was appointed to all manner of offices, and I was with you. I did not forsake you or cause your heart any sorrow. . . . Behold, when I commanded the foot soldiers of Pharaoh, together with his chariot force, I did cause you to come that they might fall down before you, and they brought all manner of good things to present to you. . . . When you were ill with the sickness I went to the Chief Physician and he made you your medicine, he did everything that you said he should do. When I had to accompany Pharaoh on his journey to the south, my thoughts were with you, and I spent those eight months without caring to eat or drink. When I returned to Memphis, I besought [begged] the Pharaoh and betook myself [came] to you, and I greatly mourned for you with the people of my house."

The Step Pyramid, built for Djoser during the 3rd Dynasty, is the oldest surviving stone structure in the world.

Over time, designs changed and rulers began building smooth-sided pyramids. Each had a rectangular base and four flat, triangular faces that met in a point at the top. The first ruler to build such a pyramid was Snefru, the founder of the 4th Dynasty. His pyramid was much larger than Djoser's. And Snefru's son, Khufu, built the largest of all in 2560 B.C. It was called the Great Pyramid.

The Great Pyramid

When completed, the Great Pyramid soared nearly five hundred feet above the desert floor and covered more than thirteen acres, which is about the size of ninety football fields. The Great Pyramid was made up of more than two million stone blocks, and assembled by laborers without the aid of beasts of burden, spe-cialized tools, or even the wheel. As French scholar Jean-Francois Champollion said, "No people whether of the old world or of the new, has had such a sublime, vast, and grandiose [unbelievably grand] conception of the art of building as the ancient Egyptians."[16]

Historians believe it took up to one hundred thousand workers twenty years to build the Great Pyramid. Most of the people who formed ancient Egypt's construction crews were peasants who worked on the pyramids during the Nile flood when they could not cultivate the fields. In addition, scribes, surveyors, engineers, carpenters, and stonecutters also worked on the pyramids. No slaves were used until much later, after Egypt's pharaohs had built an empire and brought back many prisoners of war.

Once the pyramid site was chosen, the workers turned to finding and transport-

The three pyramids at Giza, which include the Great Pyramid, dominate the Egyptian landscape. They stand today as a symbol of ancient Egypt's grandeur.

ing the stone. Some was granite cut four hundred miles to the south at Aswan. Highly trained craftsworkers used simple stone and copper tools to cut huge blocks. It was such hard work that they were organized in construction gangs with nicknames like the "Enduring Gang" and the "Vigorous Gang." Once shaped, the blocks, each of which often weighed up to 2.5 tons, or 5,000 pounds, were placed on wooden sleds and tied down with ropes. The sleds were pulled to the Nile over a path paved with logs. There they were placed on special barges filled with sand and floated to the tomb site, where they were unloaded and pulled up huge ramps to each new level of the pyramid.

These great pyramids looming against the sky symbolized the way the pharaohs of the Old Kingdom dominated all aspects of life in ancient Egypt. Through their autocratic control of the government, as well as their religious authority, they decided Egypt's political and economic direction, its religious rituals, and even which Egyptians would be granted the privilege of journeying to the afterlife. Perhaps nowhere was their influence more evident than in Memphis, the great capital of Egypt during the Old Kingdom.

Chapter

3 Egyptian Society in Old Kingdom Memphis

To maintain Egyptian unity, Menes, as its first ruler, had built a new capital twenty miles south of present-day Cairo on the border between Upper and Lower Egypt. Initially named Ineh-hedj, or "White Wall," because of the whitewashed mud-brick walls that surrounded the king's palace, the city came to be called Memphis. From this royal capital the all-powerful pharaohs of the Old Kingdom ruled the nation and brought Egypt to the peak of its power and prestige. As one ancient source commented, "The like of Memphis has never been seen."[17]

At the Head of Society

Historians cannot be certain exactly what Memphis was like because the cities of ancient Egypt, unlike its temples and tombs, were made of perishable wood and mud brick and have largely disappeared. But some scholars have reconstructed a picture of early Egyptian urban life. They believe that people of all classes—nobles, priests, government officials, skilled artisans, and common laborers—lived in the royal capital. No matter what their social class, however, the lives of the Egyptians in Memphis, as elsewhere, revolved around the pharaoh.

The pharaoh and his family lived in a great palace in the heart of the city, surrounded by Menes' thick wall. The structure, made of wood and mud brick, was light and airy, and there were fewer furnishings than might be found in modern-day palaces. There were chairs with legs in the shape of lions' paws, chests of ebony inlaid with ivory for clothing and jewels, and narrow beds with decorated footboards. And the glint of gold could be seen everywhere.

The floors, walls, and ceilings were made of plaster and covered with painted scenes of Egyptian life. Floors might be covered with lagoons full of fish and water lilies, walls decorated with papyrus reeds from which wild geese were about to take flight, and ceilings might look like the night sky over Egypt. Some scenes also may have illustrated the life of the royal family, as well as the might of the pharaoh.

Each member of the royal family had his or her own suite of rooms, supported by a staff of servants. Because of their divine blood, the members of the royal family were required to appear before their people elaborately dressed as gods or goddesses, so their appearance consumed a great deal of their time. The pharaoh's morning, for example, began with a bath in a beautiful alabaster tub. This was not merely a bath, however, but an important ritual witnessed by a number of courtiers and attendants. This ceremony was part of a system of court etiquette that became more elaborate over time. Just being present was a privilege and an indication of rank.

Egyptologist James Henry Breasted describes this system:

> Every need of the royal person was represented by some palace lord, whose duty it was to supply it, and who bore a corresponding title, like the court physician or the leader of the court music. Although the royal toilet was comparatively simple, yet a small army of wig-makers, sandal-makers, perfumers, launderers, bleachers and guardians of the royal wardrobe, filled the king's chambers.[18]

Once dressed in fine linen, the pharaoh put on his crown and other symbols of his office, then moved to the throne room to conduct the business of state. The queen and the royal princes and princesses went to their individual suites, where they mingled with courtiers and entertained special requests.

The Great Royal Wife, or the principal wife of the pharaoh, was politically the most powerful woman in the land. Her children were the direct heirs to the throne. But the pharaoh typically had a number of wives and concubines, who also bore him children and lived at the palace. If the ruler had no sons by his queen, one of his daughters would be married to the son of a secondary wife. Egyptians had no taboos preventing royal relatives from marrying one another. They believed that intermarriage kept the divine blood pure and strengthened the dynasty's hold on the throne.

Power and Roles

Many of the nobles lived in the "suburbs" of Memphis. A number of historians believe they resided in beautiful wood and mud-brick villas. Enclosed by high walls, each villa had its own garden containing a pool filled with fish and covered with lotus flowers. At one end of the pool was a small religious shrine, where the family worshiped.

Fine furniture, though not quite as fine as that enjoyed by the pharaoh, adorned the rooms of the villa. In the great reception hall, which was the main living room, the walls and the wooden pillars that supported the flat roof were decorated with scenes of Egyptian life. Thick rugs covered the floor. Such houses even had indoor bathing chambers, where servants rinsed off noble bathers, and adjacent lavatories, consisting of brick seats over removable pots.

After rising, a typical noble family breakfasted on wine, fruit, and bread filled with spices, honey, and dates. Then, the men went to work for the pharaoh at court, where they served as his most powerful and important officials. For example, the official with the title of "The Eyes and Ears of the King" was responsible for making confidential inquiries for the pharaoh. Some assisted the vizier with his many duties. For example, a noble might accompany the vizier on a visit to the provinces or serve him in his capacity as chief judge.

Ancient Egyptian society was male dominated. But women in Egypt, espe-

and several assistants, and a temporary staff of priests who served for one month three times a year. Later, some of the major temples had huge permanent staffs.

Ritual cleanliness was required of all who were actively on temple duty. According to Herodotus, "The priests shave their bodies all over every other day to guard against the presence of lice or anything else equally unpleasant while they are about their duties."[20]

The temple priests performed important religious rituals on behalf of the pharaoh, who was theoretically the only one who could interact directly with the gods. These rituals included bathing the statue of Ptah, changing its clothing, and bringing it offerings of food. Egyptologist Adolf Erman states:

> Whether it was Amon or Isis, Ptah, or the deceased [the dead pharaoh] to whom divine honors were being paid, we always find that fresh rouge and fresh robes were placed upon the divine statue and that the sacred chapel in which it was kept was cleansed and filled with perfume.[21]

Much of the food used for the sacred offerings was grown on land the pharaoh had given to the temple so it could support and pay tribute to Ptah. So, in addition to supervising rituals, the priests also had to oversee the temple's estate. Besides the products Ptah received from these lands, the pharaoh also contributed an additional portion of his revenues—grain, wine, oil, and honey—collected in taxes and from his royal estates.

Periodically, the priests organized religious festivals to honor Ptah, generally celebrating some important event in the myth of the god. Priestesses, usually women of high rank who were related in some way to government officials, participated by dancing and playing musical instruments. Bakers, brewers, butchers, and cooks who worked for the temple labored day and night to prepare food, and artisans in temple workshops created other offerings for the god.

All of these gifts were presented "for the sake of the life, prosperity, and health"[22] of the pharaoh. After the ceremony, people attending a festival could share in the food offerings, which were at other times eaten by priests and temple workers. As part of the festival, the statue of Ptah was placed in a sacred boat and carried to an altar outside the temple. This allowed the people of Memphis to worship Ptah and also ask the god questions, which they believed the statue answered by causing the boat to sway in a certain direction.

Egyptian Astronomers

Egyptian priests wanted religious festivals to coincide with days that also were critical to Egypt's agricultural success—days of flooding, days of planting, and days of harvesting. So the priests had to invent a scientific way to keep track of time. To that end, Egypt's priest-astronomers studied the stars, plotting their courses and those of the planets. Eventually, they noticed that the brightest star in the sky, today known as Sirius, began to appear above the eastern horizon just before the floods came. The period of time between one rising of Sirius and the next was 365 days. Once the astronomers knew this, they developed a calendar of 365 days with 12

How Do I Look?

Almost all ancient Egyptians spent a lot of time on their appearance. Though they wore wigs, they were extremely concerned about their hair. Egyptologist Adolf Erman describes this concern in Life in Ancient Egypt.

"Men as well as women required of him [the doctor] that when their hair came out he should make it grow again, as well as restore the black colour of youth to their white locks. . . . As a remedy against the hair turning white the head was to be 'anointed with the blood of a black calf that had been boiled with oil.' As a preservative against the same misfortune, the 'blood of the horn of the black bull,' also boiled with oil, was to be used as an ointment. . . . In these prescriptions the black colour of the bull's hair was . . . supposed to pass into the hair of the human being. . . . When the hair fell out, it could be renewed by six kinds of fat worked up together into a pomade [perfumed ointment]—the fat of the lion, of the hippopotamus, of the crocodile, of the cat, of the snake, and of the ibex [wild goat]. It was also considered as really strengthening to the hair to anoint it with the 'tooth of a donkey crushed in honey.'"

A detail from an 18th Dynasty wall painting depicts guests at a banquet. The women wear elaborate gowns, jewelry, and dark wigs.

Egyptian druggists squeeze an animal skin filled with medicinal herbs into a vase.

months grouped into 3 seasons of 120 days each—flood, planting, harvest. Each month had 30 days, each week had 10 days, and each day had 24 hours. The extra five days were used as festivals for the five principal Egyptian gods. Modified later, however, it formed the basis for our modern calendar.

Doctors and Druggists

The world's first doctors and druggists also lived in Memphis during the Old Kingdom. Renowned for their excellence, and praised by Greek poet Homer in his epic *Odyssey*, Egyptian physicians were more skilled than any other doctors in the ancient world.

A man who wanted to become a doctor had to either study with an established physician—often his father—or attend a medical school attached to a temple. Once their study was completed, many Egyptian doctors established themselves in general practice, treating all kinds of illnesses. But some became the first skilled specialists, or doctors who studied a particular part of the body. Modern scholars have found evidence to support the existence of such specialization. P. G. Sobhy Bey of Egypt states:

> In the tomb of the pyramid period a skull was found showing clear evidence of a successful operation for drainage of an abscess [infection] at the root of the first molar. Another skull showed two teeth skillfully tied together with gold wire, evidently to fasten a loose tooth to its more stable neighbor and so to prevent it falling out.[23]

"He Has a Very Thick Skull"

A wounded officer in the pharaoh's charioteers named Senmut was carried by his friend Kenamun to the tent of the ruler's chief physician. Leonard Cottrell, in Life Under the Pharaohs, *describes his medical care.*

"First the physician cleans out the arrow wounds, staunches [stops] the flow of blood and neatly stitches the severed flesh. He makes a careful examination and finds that Senmut's left arm and leg are paralysed. He examines the abrasion on the skull, ascertains that there is no fracture, but recognizes that the paralysis is due to pressure on the brain which must be relieved. His surgical instruments lie on a table beside the bed: curved knives of various shapes, drills and saws. With a small sharp saw, he removes a portion of the skull and cuts away the membrane so that the brain lies exposed. Delicately removing the clotted blood and cleaning the damaged tissues, he stitches the membrane back in place, replaces the piece of skull and binds it in position with bandages and adhesive. It is already dawn when he rises to his feet. . . . In answer to Kenamun's unspoken question, the doctor says 'I cannot say. It is too early to tell. . . . His heart is good. He may survive. But he cannot be moved for a long time. He must stay here for some weeks; then perhaps he can be moved to Kadesh.' Smiling at Kenamun's anxious face, he drops his hand on the young man's shoulder and remarks: 'Don't worry, my son. Like all you soldiers, he has a very thick skull.'"

Egyptian doctors also developed a written manual of medical practice that covered such subjects as anatomy, general illnesses, eye ailments, gynecology (study of the diseases of women), stomach conditions, the action of the heart and its vessels, as well as how to use surgery to treat wounds and fractures. The rolls of papyrus that contain this information are generally considered the world's first medical books.

Egyptian medical books also discussed drugs, which Egyptian doctors used frequently. In fact, Egyptians were the first to practice pharmacy, the art of preparing and distributing drugs. They were the first to use several present-day drugs, including opium. They also developed many sound herbal remedies, some of which are still available today. Castor oil, for example, was administered for indigestion, much as it was earlier in this century.

Doctors in Egypt performed the first successful experiments in surgery as early as 3000 B.C. Through mummification, the

Egyptians had learned much a[bout]
human body. In order to embal[m]
they had to remove most of th[e]
organs. As they discovered th[e]
and the nature of these organs
tians probably made the first [...]
in anatomy. This knowledge h[elped]
in performing surgery on liv[ing]
and contributed to the gro[wth of medi-]
cine. Not limiting themsel[ves]
complaints, Egyptian doctor[s]
ous head wounds and eve[n]
spinal injuries, and they w[ould]
use splints to set broken bon[es].

When they were abou[t to perform]
surgery, doctors like Imho[tep, archi-]
tect of the Great Pyramid[...]
patients a special drink [...]
kill the pain. Then, to r[...]
they would wash up and [...in-]
struments in a fire.

A Path to Adv[ancement]

Unlike doctors, most [...]
learned to read or writ[e...]
boys attended special s[chools...]
trained to become scrib[es...]
ers. Usually, the child[ren...]
tend such schools were [...]
families. Most were th[e...]
Sometimes, however, the [...]
was chosen. Girls were n[ot...]
the scribe schools. They u[sed...]
at home learning dome[stic...]
their mothers until they [...]
was sometimes as early as [...]
or thirteen.

Once enrolled, the p[upils...]
sic reading, writing, and [...]
about ten years and then tr[...]

[Wor]kshops

[...]g carpenters, met[al-]
[...work]ers, and sculptors,
[...]l level in the royal
[...re]ceived their train-
[...]ed to someone al[ready skilled in a]
particular craft.
[...]d from father to [son...]
[...]e poor section of
[...]rk shortly after
[...]the busy work-
[...]ace or to one of

By the Old Kingdom, Egyptian carpenters already possessed simple versions of almost all the tools used by modern carpenters. They used these tools to produce furniture made from local wood and reeds as well as more expensive pieces from imported cedar. Carpenters also made coffins for tombs, shrines for the gods, wooden pillars used in building, and boats for travel and sacred ceremonies. They used wooden pegs instead of nails to join pieces of wood.

Metalworkers practiced one of the most highly developed crafts in ancient Egypt. They made everything from tools and weapons to statues of the gods to exquisite necklaces, bracelets, and earrings. Gold for craft manufacture was first weighed, then given to goldsmiths, who melted the metal and poured it into molds. The hardened form was hammered into shape and finally weighed again to make sure none of the metal had been stolen.

Because the Egyptians had no diamonds, rubies, emeralds, or sapphires, jewelers embellished the necklaces and other items produced by goldsmiths for the pharaoh and his nobles with such semiprecious stones as purple amethyst, green malachite, orange carnelian, deep blue lapis lazuli, and blue-green turquoise. For the less wealthy, jewelers made simpler pieces, using copper, shells, and faience, a glaze of powdered quartz.

Weavers produced Egyptian clothing from linen because cotton was unknown in ancient Egypt. Much of it was produced for the upper classes and the royal family. Egyptologist Adolf Erman testifies to its extraordinary quality:

> They lavished all their skill in the one endeavor [attempt] to prepare the finest and whitest linen that was possible, and they certainly brought their linen to great perfection; I need only remind my readers of the white garments worn by men of rank, which were so fine that their limbs could be seen gleaming through them. Some of this very fine linen we possess is almost comparable to our silken materials for smoothness and softness.[25]

Sculptors shaped limestone, granite, and alabaster into pillars and statues for palaces, temples, and tombs. They worked with copper chisels and mallets, constantly

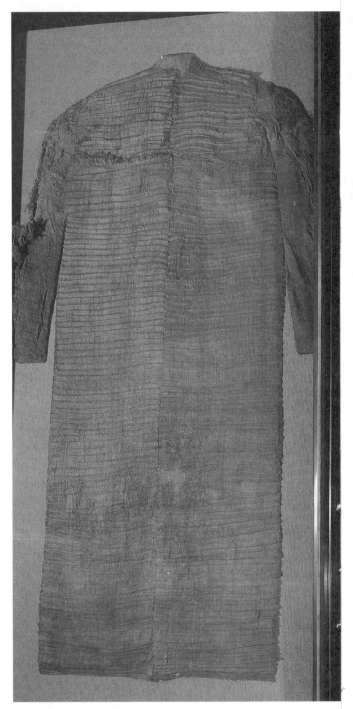

This pleated linen robe, found in a 12th Dynasty tomb, most likely belonged to a member of a royal family.

Vase makers add the finishing touches to a piece of pottery. In the Egyptian social hierarchy, artisans were below nobles, priests, and government officials.

their homes and hurried to their duties for the pharaoh. They usually worked from dawn to dusk, performing back-breaking physical labor of all kinds.

Some worked on the docks, unloading boats carrying all sorts of cargoes, including vegetables from the Delta, livestock and grain from Upper Egypt, and cedar logs from Byblos in Phoenicia, as well as ivory, ebony, and gold from the land of Nubia to the south. Others worked at mak-

ing and stacking mud bricks that would be used in building and maintaining houses, palaces, and the walls surrounding the city.

Memphis was the hub of Old Kingdom culture. Supremely confident in their pharaoh, everyone—from the lowest laborer working in the fields to the metal-worker creating fine jewelry to high-ranking nobles and officials—devoted their labor and their lives to his service. But things were about to change.

4 Chaos Reigns in Egypt

Ruling from Memphis, the pharaohs of the Old Kingdom had total control over Egypt's political, economic, and religious life. Supremely confident of their absolute power, they did not dream of a time when they would no longer control their country. They were about to come face to face, however, with that realization. After centuries of unparalleled progress, the Old Kingdom was about to come to an end, and chaos would reign in Egypt for more than 150 years, from 2200 to 2040 B.C.

A Time of Desperation

Around the end of the Old Kingdom, the climate in Egypt slowly began to change. Less rain and snow fell in the mountains of central Africa, and there were a number of low floods. Lower flood levels meant that less of the rich soil was deposited on the plain at the river's edge. As a result, fewer fields were cultivated, and harvests decreased in size or were less abundant. Stored supplies dwindled, and famine began to stalk the land. The people of all classes were affected, but the peasants were especially hard hit. In one pyramid of the time, scenes of skeletal men sucking their fingers in their desperate hunger were carved on the stone walls.

Mobs continually roamed the countryside trying to find food. One Egyptian nomarch, or district governor, reported, "Upper Egypt in its entirety was dying of hunger, everybody eating his children."[27] Experts doubt that the writer actually meant that Egyptians were eating their children, but was rather underlining the seriousness of the situation.

As people watched their families starve, they grew angry and demanded that the pharaoh do something to alleviate their hunger. They wanted him to intercede with the gods—as he always had done—to control the river, the sun, and the soil. This time, however, the gods, or nature, did not cooperate. Year after year, conditions in the country deteriorated. People began to lose faith in the pharaoh as a god. The fact that the rulers of the time were very weak only accelerated their rebelliousness.

Lawlessness grew as mobs became more violent in their search for food, and the pharaohs in Memphis did nothing to restore order. Because the rulers' power had declined, they could not force the increasingly independent nomarchs to provide soldiers for a temporary army to meet the crisis as they had in the past. With no relief in sight, Egypt plunged deeper into lawlessness.

A wooden statue of an emaciated man holding a bowl is testament to the widespread famine at the end of the Old Kingdom.

One ancient author described what it was like during this desperate time in Egypt:

> The door-keepers say: "Let us go plunder." The washerman refuses to carry his load. . . . A man looks upon his son as an enemy. . . . A man goes to plough with his shield. Poor men now possess fine things. He who once made for himself no sandals now possesses riches. . . . The high-born are full of lamentations [complaints], and the poor are full of joy. Every town says, "Let us drive out the powerful from our midst." . . . It is grief that walks through the land. . . . Great and small say: "I wish I were dead!" . . . They who had clothes are now in rags. He who wove not for himself now possesses fine linen. . . . He who had no bread now possesses a barn. . . . She who looked at her face in the water now possesses a mirror. . . . No office is any longer in its right place: they are a frightened herd without herdsmen [strong rulers].[28]

Hungry Egyptians murdered their neighbors for a loaf of bread and robbed the houses of many nobles. Hatred between lower and upper classes intensified. Then, the people did something they would never have dared to do before. They robbed and desecrated some of the magnificent tombs and funeral temples of the Old Kingdom pharaohs. They smashed the old rulers' statues and tore apart their mummies to rip the jewelry from their bodies. With these riches, they had a chance to buy food.

The Decline of Royal Power

The escalating violence further undermined the authority of the pharaoh, and the state became even less stable. Gradually, huge building projects were abandoned because the ruler did not have the power to summon the vast number of men needed. Nor could his diminishing coffers provide the huge quantities of food and clothing necessary to afford them. The pharaohs continued to construct smaller tombs, using the few laborers they still

Death Is Before Me Today

With the demise of the Old Kingdom life became so chaotic and violent that many people felt hopeless. One man, in The Dispute of a Man With His Ba *[soul], quoted in Nicholas Grimal's* A History of Ancient Egypt, *spoke of death as a release from the situation.*

"To Whom shall I speak today?
Brothers are mean,
The friends of today do not love.
To whom shall I speak today?
Hearts are greedy,
Everyone robs his comrade's goods.
(To whom shall I speak today?)
Kindness has perished,
Insolence assaults everyone.
To whom shall I speak today?
One is content with evil,
Goodness is cast to the ground everywhere.

Death is before me today
(Like) a sick man's recovery,
Like going outdoors after confinement.
Death is before me today
Like the fragrance of myrrh,
Like sitting under sail on breeze day . . . .
Death is before me today
Like a well-trodden way,
Like a man's coming home from warfare.
Death is before me today
Like the clearing of the sky,
As when a man discovers what he ignored.
Death is before me today
Like a man's longing to see his home
When he has spent many years in captivity."

controlled in Memphis and its immediate vicinity. The diminishing size of their pyramids was an outward symbol of the gradual decline of royal power.

Eventually, the pharaoh could no longer carry on the business of Egypt. Scholars believe that foreign trade with Byblos and Nubia, which only the pharaoh had the right to conduct, stopped. Mining of valuable turquoise and copper came to a halt. Raids by nomadic desert tribes, always troublesome but usually controlled by border patrols, became more frequent as the central authority weakened.

The Gods on Their Side

Along with the economic collapse, the growing power of the priests also weakened the power of the pharaoh. Over time, as worship of the sun god increased, the priests of Re grew more numerous and more powerful. Pharaohs seeking to appease them lavished gifts of produce from the state storehouses or estates on temples in both the capital and throughout the provinces. Huge amounts of food could pass through a single temple in a given year. For example, the yearly total for one temple was 7,720 loaves of bread, 1,002 oxen, and 1,000 geese, along with assorted bread, beer, and cakes.

In time, to win the favor of the gods, the pharaohs expanded their offerings even more, donating large tracts of land in the form of estates to the temples, especially to the temples of Re. A single donation might be as large as five hundred acres. These lands supplied the temple with produce for offerings. The gradual shift in the ownership of land and produce from the pharaoh to the temples made them increasingly independent economically.

In addition to these direct gifts, the pharaoh also decreed that the temples did not have to pay taxes or provide laborers for any state projects. One pharaoh's decree made this policy clear:

My Majesty does not allow that they [temple personnel] are put to work . . . on farms of cattle, donkeys, and small cattle [sheep and goats] . . . or any forced labor or any tax which may be

To appease the priests, pharaohs bestowed huge gifts on the temples. Consequently, the temples' estates grew and the priests became even more powerful. Here, a pharaoh, accompanied by a priest, inspects his tomb.

imposed by crown property . . . for the length of eternity. [29]

Because of these policies, the temples' estates kept growing. With more land and no taxes to pay, these estates could accumulate greater wealth. The ruler, of course, had less to pay artisans and laborers working for the central government.

As the temples grew stronger and richer, the priests of Re seized the opportunity to wrest more power for themselves and further limit the pharaoh's influence. Knowing that the ruler's divinity enhanced his political power, the priests openly declared that the pharaoh was to be viewed from this point on as the *human* son of Re. In one stroke, they redefined the pharaoh's image. Although created by the god, he was no longer the actual child of Re and a god himself.

The people believed the priests and lost even more respect for the pharaoh. Before long, the estates of Re's temples emerged as small, independent states. In theory, the people living in these states were still subject to the pharaoh, but in reality the priests were their rulers.

Officials Gain Independence

The increasing independence of important government officials also contributed significantly to the decline in the pharaoh's power in Egypt, primarily through their gradual acquisition of more land—at the pharaoh's expense. In ancient Egypt, it was the ruler's responsibility to provide his key officials with land and

At the end of the Old Kingdom, government officials grew wealthier and more powerful, while the pharaohs' influence waned. Here, an official checks the weight of rings of gold.

Tale of the Eloquent Peasant

After the Old Kingdom, officials often grew more corrupt. In the Tale of the Eloquent Peasant, *quoted in Nicholas Grimal's* A History of Ancient Egypt, *a greedy government official uses trickery to seize a peasant's belongings. The terrified peasant pleads for justice.*

"Oh high steward, my lord, greatest of the great, leader of all! When you go down to the sea of justice and sail it with a fair wind, no squall shall strip away your sail, nor will your boat be idle. . . . You will not founder when you touch land, no flood will carry you away. You will not taste the river's evils, you will not see a frightened face. Fish will come darting to you, fattened fowl surround you. For you are father to the orphan, husband to the widow, brother to the rejected woman, apron to the motherless. . . . Leader free of greed, great man free of baseness, destroyer of falsehood, creator of rightness. . . . When I speak, may you hear! Do justice, oh praised one, who is praised by the praised; remove my grief, I am burdened."

construction materials for their tombs, as well as supplies of produce to be used for the performance of continued religious rituals after death. As with the temples, the rulers found it easier to award officials land rather than send them produce. In this way, subordinates could be responsible for supplying their own tombs by growing crops on their new lands. The pharaohs also declared that, like the temples' lands, these "funeral estates" did not have to pay taxes.

Many important officials received property when they were appointed to office in addition to lands awarded for their funeral estates. In ancient Egypt, the pharaoh ceded great estates, along with people and livestock, to each important official for his lifetime. The official was expected to use this land to support his family and any subordinates who reported to

him, and usually to pay taxes. These lands were supposed to be given back to the pharaoh when the official died. Some heirs, however, began keeping the land for themselves.

Great Lords Act Like Pharaohs

Up to this point, most of the land had been owned by the pharaoh and was considered state, rather than private, property. However, gradually the lands acquired by each official formed the core of an increasingly larger private estate. The officials grew progressively wealthier, while the ruler, minus his lands and the crops they produced, became poorer. This whole process was compounded as the

A painting from a tomb wall depicts a city governor and a vizier among Egyptian women. As government officials gained more independence, they began to act more like pharaohs, setting up their own courts and employing officials.

number of officials on the pharaoh's payroll grew.

Officials both at court and in the provinces were also gaining independence from the pharaoh because the way in which they acquired their positions changed. Originally, important government officials were appointed by the pharaoh. This made them dependent on him and kept them somewhat in check, for the pharaoh could replace them. Now, officials tried to get the law changed so that their positions would become hereditary, a father would be able to pass a position on to his son.

Although they were unsuccessful and the original law remained on the books, many officials, including both the vizier and the nomarchs, simply behaved as if their offices were hereditary. This meant that they could do as they pleased. Though frustrated, the pharaohs at Memphis could do little to stop this trend because they were weak and lacked power to enforce the law.

In the provinces, the nomarchs, whose ancestors were the chiefs of the Predynastic Period, had inherited a tradition of independence. Now, after seizing the right to pass on their rule to their sons, they began acting like pharaohs instead of loyal servants to the pharaoh and the central government. Demanding to be addressed as "great lord," these princes began establishing their power bases, setting up elaborate courts that employed many officials.

During the many years that Egypt was in chaos, these local rulers also tried to enhance their power by helping the subjects in their districts to prosper. They could not do anything about poor weather, but they managed their lands well and stored adequate supplies for emergencies. One nomarch described some of the techniques he used to ensure the contentment of his subjects:

I was rich in grain. When the land was in need I maintained the city with kha and heket [grain measures], I allowed the citizen to fetch for himself grain; and his wife, the widow and her son. I remitted [cancelled] all imposts [unpaid debts] which I found counted by my fathers. I filled the pastures with cattle, every man had many breeds, the cows brought forth twofold, the folds were full of calves. [30]

Many of these local rulers were contemptuous of the pharaoh, who could not seem to do anything to help Egypt's problems. One described his lack of respect for Egypt's ruler, saying, "I rescued my city in the day of violence from the terrors of the royal house." [31]

Finally, many of the nomarchs were also chief priests to the local gods, which further solidified their newly gained political and economic power, partly because they received double portions of land from the pharaoh in their capacity as government officials and priests. Also, in time some nomarchs came to be viewed as gods themselves, much as the early district tribal chiefs had been. They declared that they no longer needed the pharaoh to guide them into the afterlife. And they began to construct extravagant tombs near those of their ancestors in cemeteries near the provincial capitals—the centers of their power—rather than near the tombs of the weakening pharaohs.

Two Sets of Pharaohs

The nomarchs also began to assemble private armies, manned with full-time soldiers instead of the untrained peasants generally provided to the pharaoh during times of national emergency. These new private troops were usually mercenaries, or hired soldiers, from Nubia. The nomarchs used these armies to extend their power within Egypt. And just as early tribal chiefs had done, the nomarchs soon began to fight each other.

During this period, alliances were made and broken and violent clashes occurred. Egypt resembled medieval Europe under the feudal system, where power was decentralized as rival barons battled for territory, largely unchecked by weak national kings. Over time, the rulers of Herakleopolis, the 20th Nome of Upper Egypt, emerged as the strongest of many; the nomarchs there were strong rulers and Herakleopolis enjoyed a good strategic position, just south of the Delta between Upper and Lower Egypt.

In 2160 B.C., the nomarch of Herakleopolis, Meribre Khety I, suddenly proclaimed himself pharaoh of Egypt and seized the throne from the weak 8th Dynasty kings who still ruled Memphis and the surrounding area. Meribre Khety I then founded the 9th Dynasty, and he and his successors began to try to restore order and to extend their authority in Egypt.

The pharaohs of Herakleopolis were aided by their chief ally, the local ruler of Asyut, the 13th Nome of Upper Egypt, which lay to the south about halfway between Herakleopolis and Thebes. The modern city of Asyut stands on the ruins of the provincial capital of the same name. The prince of Asyut described how his lands had improved in the more stable atmosphere:

Every official was at his post, there was no one fighting, nor any shooting an arrow. The child was not smitten beside its mother, nor the citizen beside his wife. There was no evil doer . . . nor anyone doing violence against his house. . . . When night came, he who slept on the road gave me praise, for he was like a man in his house; the fear of my soldier was his protection.[32]

However, the pharaohs of Herakleopolis and their allies could not subdue the entire country, at least not for long. A family of nomarchs who ruled the 4th Nome of Thebes was rapidly gaining power in Upper Egypt. They managed to get control of the area around Thebes and set up an independent kingdom there. Then, they led the south in a rebellion against the pharaohs of Herakleopolis. To reach them, however, the Thebans had to march through Asyut, and when they tried, they were served a devastating defeat by the local ruler and his formidable army.

Flush with victory, the prince described how he defeated the Theban leader and smashed the rebellion:

I went forth against him with only one small regiment, and so soundly beat him that he left off the battle as though he were in terror, and the nome of Asyut returned like a bull which attacks a pack of dogs. There was no peace for me until I had beaten them down. The leader of the southerners went into battle in beautiful clothes, but he fell into the water, his ship went aground, and his army, like ducks, fled before the hunter. I set fire to their vessel, and the flames shot up higher than the mast. I had overcome him who had risen in rebellion . . . and I could then say to the chief of Upper Egypt: "Listen," and be sure that he would harken [listen] to me.[33]

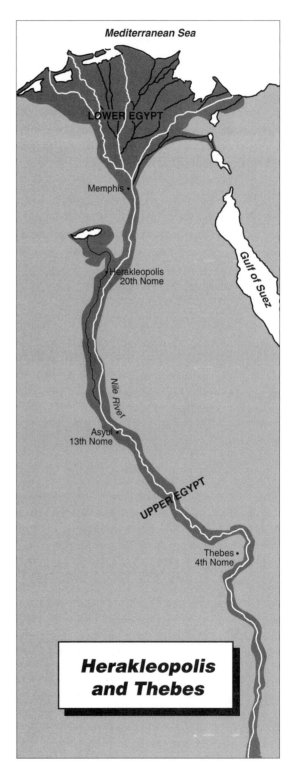

Mediterranean Sea

LOWER EGYPT

Memphis

Herakleopolis
20th Nome

Gulf of Suez

Nile River

Asyut
13th Nome

UPPER EGYPT

Thebes
4th Nome

Herakleopolis and Thebes

Prince Against Prince

The conflict between the princes of Herakleopolis and Thebes went on for some time. Ankhtifi was one of the chief allies of Herakleopolis. Quoted in Nicholas Grimal's A History of Ancient Egypt, *he describes some aspects of the conflict and brags about his part in it.*

"I was the man who found the solution when it was lacking in the country thanks to poor decisions, and my speech was clever and my bravery won the day. . . . I am an honest man who has no equal, a man who can talk freely when others are obliged to be silent. At a time when it was necessary to shake off fear, Upper Egypt was silent [the other nomes were too afraid to stand up against Thebes]. . . .

I then went down to the country to the west of Armant [town near Thebes where most battles were fought] and I found that all the forces of Thebes and Koptos [an ally of Thebes] had attacked the fortresses of Armant. . . . I reached the west bank of the Theban province. . . . Then my courageous crack troops . . . ventured to the west and the east of the Theban nome, looking for an open battle. But no one dared to come out from Thebes because they were afraid of my troops. . . . The whole of Upper Egypt died of hunger. . . . But I refused to see anyone die of hunger in this province. I arranged for grain to be loaned to Upper Egypt. . . . And I do not think that anything like this has been done by the provincial governors who came before me."

However, this battle was just the first of many clashes between these two warring powers. Before long, Egypt was split into two areas controlled by two sets of self-proclaimed pharaohs. One set—Dynasties 9 and 10—ruled from Herakleopolis. The other—Dynasty 11—ruled from Thebes.

During this period, Herakleopolis and Thebes exerted varying degrees of control over their respective areas. They still had to contend with the ambitious, battling lords heading the many small states that had grown up around temples and in the provinces throughout Egypt. The highly centralized state of the Old Kingdom had completely deteriorated. And after nearly one thousand years of progress under strong pharaohs, Egypt was divided into kingdoms similar to those that had existed before the nation was formed. Weary of the chaos, most Egyptians longed for the return of an all-powerful pharaoh and the order that kind of ruler brought. The Thebans were about to help them get what they wanted.

5 The Middle Kingdom: A New Egypt Arises

The period of social chaos and civil war finally came to an end when the kings of the 11th Dynasty of Thebes triumphed over the rulers of Herakleopolis. They again united the Delta and the Nile Valley into one state and brought peace to Egypt. They began what is known as the Middle Kingdom, which lasted from 2040 until 1674 B.C. Although Middle Kingdom rulers were able to restore Egypt to some of its lost splendor, both the monarchy and the country had changed. For the rest of ancient Egypt's history, its pharaohs would be trying to recapture the past.

The Triumph of Thebes

Over time, the 11th Dynasty rulers at Thebes became more powerful. By the time Nebhepetre Mentuhotep II became ruler in 2061 B.C., the lands he controlled stretched from the first cataract near Aswan in the south almost to the border of Asyut in the north. Despite this vast empire, Nebhepetre Mentuhotep II sought to expand his territory, but Asyut—the strong ally of Herakleopolis—stood in his way. Events in another nome, Thinnis, the 8th Nome of Upper Egypt, provided Mentuhotep with the opportunity he had been waiting for.

Thinnis, which was under the control of Herakleopolis, was plagued by famine but had received no help from the pharaoh there. So the prince of Thinnis revolted against him. Allied with Herakleopolis, the prince of Asyut immediately sent his army to put down the rebellion. While the prince was occupied with Thinnis's revolt, Mentuhotep stormed into Asyut with his troops. He captured the capital city—which, with the prince absent in Thinnis, fell without much of a struggle—and then was able to take control of the rest of the nome. With the fall of Asyut, the 10th Dynasty of Herakleopolis soon collapsed. In triumph, Mentuhotep II proclaimed himself pharaoh of a united Egypt.

Having won his position in battle, the new pharaoh had yet to solidify his authority over the whole nation. His power, though greater than the other nomarchs', was still more limited than that of Old Kingdom pharaohs. He first reestablished the central government at Thebes—his home-town and the new capital of Egypt—by setting up the departments and the position of vizier that the pharaohs of the Old Kingdom had created.

Then, Mentuhotep turned his attention toward the provinces. Those princes of Upper Egypt who had remained loyal to

ing temples and tombs that had been destroyed during the period of chaos and building new ones. Mentuhotep also began to construct his own pyramid, which, though smaller, was modeled after those built during the Old Kingdom.

Extending Egypt's Borders

Once more in command of a sizable army with soldiers provided by local rulers, Mentuhotep was able to defend and extend Egypt's boundaries. He sent troops to police the borders and personally led several expeditions against nomadic tribes in Libya and the Sinai Peninsula, who continued to stage lightning raids against Egypt. The pharaoh and his troops also pushed back invaders from the east, called Asiatics by the Egyptians, who threatened to invade the eastern Delta. Under Mentuhotep, Egypt set out to reconquer Nubia and managed to seize control of the northern part of the nation, an area just south of Wadi Halfa in present-day northern Sudan. This action secured valuable areas for mining and trade, which once again resumed with vigor.

After fifty-two years as a king and thirty-one as pharaoh of all Egypt, Mentuhotep II died and the throne passed to his son, Mentuhotep III. With the authority of the pharaoh now well established and the border tribes under control, Mentuhotep III could send peaceful expeditions into the lands around Egypt. He ordered his vizier, Amenemhet, to mount a grand expedition to travel to the quarries of Hammamat, which lay between the Nile Valley and the Red Sea. He was searching for a special stone for his sarcophagus, as the pharaohs

Middle Kingdom ruler Mentuhotep II, depicted in a stone carving from about 2000 B.C., declared himself pharaoh of a united Egypt after the fall of the 10th Dynasty of Herakleopolis.

Mentuhotep were allowed to continue ruling their provinces, but the new pharaoh replaced the dangerously independent rulers of Asyut and Herakleopolis. In addition, Mentuhotep used his power to place officials loyal to him in the nome governments of Lower Egypt. Now, nome rulers in both Upper and Lower Egypt owed their allegiance to Mentuhotep.

To impress the people with his influence and to help unify the nation, Mentuhotep began a campaign to restore the office of pharaoh to its former greatness. He started a vast building program, restor-

The Story of Sinuhe

The Story of Sinuhe, *quoted in Nicholas Grimal's* A History of Ancient Egypt, *tells the tale of an official who—out of fear, not guilt—fled Egypt after the murder of the pharaoh Amenemhet I. Many years later, longing for his homeland, he begged for a pardon.*

"Lo, this flight which the servant made—I did not plan it. It was not in my heart. . . . I do not know what removed me from my place. It was like a dream. . . . I had not heard a reproach; my name was not heard in the mouth of the herald. Yet my flesh crept, my feet hurried, my heart drove me; the god who had willed this flight dragged me away. . . . Ra [Re] has set his fear of you throughout the land, the dread of you in every foreign country. Whether I am at the residence, whether I am at this place, it is you who covers this horizon. The sun rises at your pleasure. The water in the river is drunk when you wish. The air of heaven is breathed at your bidding. . . . One lives by the breath which you give. As Ra, Horus and Hathor [goddess of women] love your august nose, may Monthu, lord of Thebes [Theban god of war] wish it to live forever!"

were once more able to spend lavishly on their tombs.

Amenemhet managed to gather ten thousand soldiers and workers from all over the land. This huge force made the long journey through the desert and remained at the quarries for twenty-five days, subsisting on thousands of jars of water and loaves of bread provided by the pharaoh. The trip was so well organized that when it was completed Amenemhet boasted, "My soldiers returned without loss; not a man perished, not a troop was missing, not an ass died, not a workman was enfeebled [taken sick]."[34] This expedition was similar to those of the early Old Kingdom and could never have been carried out by the weak rulers of the more recent, troubled period. They would not

have had the power to marshal the workers, the soldiers, or the provisions.

A Different Kind of Pharaoh

The pharaohs of the 11th Dynasty, including Mentuhotep II and his son, prepared the way for the tremendous development in Egypt under the succeeding dynasty. Around 1991 B.C., Amenemhet I seized power, fighting off several others who claimed the throne, and founded the 12th Dynasty. To reinforce his position, the new ruler commissioned writers to compose literature that supported his claim to the throne. One ancient piece describes his coming:

A king will come from the south, called Ameni [Amenemhet], the son of a woman of Nubia, and born in Upper Egypt. He will receive the white crown and wear the red crown. . . . Be glad, you people of this time. . . . The Asiatics will fall before his carnage [massacre], and the Libyans will fall before his flame. The foes succumb [surrender] to his onset and the rebels to his might. The royal serpent [sacred symbol of the pharaoh's supreme rule] which is on his forehead pacifies the rebels. . . . And Right will come again into its place, and Iniquity [evil] will be cast out.[35]

Amenemhet ruled a united Egypt, but his power remained somewhat limited. The nomarchs, though individually weaker than the pharaoh, were still a force to be reckoned with. To maintain his position as pharaoh, Amenemhet had to make certain concessions to them. For example, like Mentuhotep II before him, Amenemhet allowed nomarchs who had backed him in his bid for the throne to continue to rule their provinces. In return, as before, they gave the pharaoh a share of the revenue from their lands and the use of their troops if he needed them.

But when any nomarch gained too much authority and became too aggressive, Amenemhet used the power he had gained to end that local governor's control over his nome. The pharaoh appointed new governors for some provinces and redrew boundary lines for others, reducing their size. To maintain a close watch over the nomarchs in the north, where he had fewer allies, Amenemhet moved the capital from Thebes to a new city near Memphis—the city of Itj-tawy, later called el-Lisht.

Meanwhile, the pharaoh built up his power base by increasing the size and strength of the central government's bureaucracy. The new officials, of course, owed their loyalty directly to him. Under Amenemhet, these officials did not have to be members of the pharaoh's family. Anyone who had learned to be a scribe could serve.

Restored Peace

Keeping power balanced among the nomarchs while increasing authority of the pharaoh helped bring order and prosperity to a newly united Egypt. One local official described the effects of Amenemhet's actions:

> His majesty . . . restored that which he found ruined; that which a city had taken from its neighbor; while he caused city to know its boundary with city, establishing their landmarks like the heavens . . . investigating according to that which was of old, because he so greatly loved justice.[36]

Besides controlling the nomarchs and bringing peace to Egypt, Amenemhet and other rulers of the 12th Dynasty won popular support by decreeing that all people who owned land could now pass it on to their children. In addition, the ruler also declared that all people, regardless of rank, now had the right to join Osiris in the afterlife.

To exercise this right, all people had to do was perform a small ceremony in which they wrote their names on a wooden tablet or a clay vase, along with the words "Osiris justified, lord of fealty [loyalty]." [37] These words, they believed, pledged them to Osiris, and gave them the same opportunities, at least after death, as the pharaoh and his nobles.

In the last ten years of his reign, Amenemhet I made his son Sesostris I coruler to make sure the succession went smoothly. The tactic helped Sesostris hold on to the throne in 1962 B.C., when Amenemhet was murdered by members of his own household. This kind of conspiracy served as a reminder to the Middle Kingdom pharaohs that their thrones were not as secure as those of the Old Kingdom rulers.

Recognizing the ever-present possibility of treachery, Amenemhet told his son how to keep his throne and his life:

Be on guard against subordinates [those of inferior position]; do not approach them, and do not be alone. Do not trust a brother or a friend—that profits nothing. If you sleep, guard your heart, for in the day of adversity [troubled times] a man has no friends. I gave to the poor and nourished the orphan; I caused him who was nothing to reach the goal, just like the man who was highborn. He who ate my food disdained [looked down upon] me. [38]

A Golden Age

Amenemhet I and his son Sesostris I laid the foundation for the golden age that Egypt experienced later in the 12th Dynasty. From 1878 to 1797 B.C., during the reigns of Sesostris III and Amenemhet III, the Middle Kingdom reached its peak. The

Egyptians conquered Nubia and many city-states in Syria and Palestine, which then sent tribute, or forced payments, to their Egyptian overlords. Trade with other lands increased as ships and caravans carried goods to and from Egypt. Improved methods of irrigation created thousands of additional acres of farmland. More and more turquoise and copper were mined, and stone by the tons was quarried. All of these activities poured wealth into the pharaoh's

Twelfth Dynasty pharaoh Sesostris III ruled during a period of remarkable cultural achievement referred to as the golden age.

The pyramid of Amenemhet III was one of the greatest architectural splendors of the pharaoh's reign. The outer casing of the pyramid is now gone, leaving the brick core of the funeral complex exposed.

treasury, which led to a burst of splendid cultural achievement.

Throughout the land, signs of this splendor were revealed in vast building projects. The most famous pyramid of the time was that of Amenemhet III. His funeral complex included an enormous temple, with huge stone columns and countless courts connected by winding passages. Herodotus later wrote about this temple, calling it a labyrinth through which no stranger could find his way. The 12th Dynasty rulers also built a number of temples dedicated to a new national deity, Amen-Re, who emerged as a combination of the sun god, Re, and Amen, the local god of Thebes.

The reigns of Sesostris III and Amenemhet III were rich in sculpture as well as architecture. Huge statues up to sixty feet tall were erected, and they were unlike statues left by previous rulers. Old Kingdom artists always showed the pharaohs as young and vigorous, no matter what their age or condition. But 12th Dynasty statues reflected the fact that the ruler was no

longer viewed as an unapproachable god. Their artists often showed the Egyptian rulers with lines of age etched on their faces. At the pharaohs' request, sculptors produced not only statues of them, but also of a host of past kings to emphasize the return to the royal tradition.

Literature also reached a peak during the golden age, partly because the art of writing was developed again as the central government began to once more carry out its functions. The pieces written during the 12th Dynasty were later used as models in Egyptian schools. One important poem was composed to honor Sesostris III:

Twice great is the king of his city, above a million arms: as for other rulers of men, they are but common folk. . . .

Twice great is the king of his city: he is . . . a bulwark, with walls built of sharp stones of Kesem [Egypt]. . . .

Twice great is the king of his city: he is as it were a shade, the cool vegetation

During the Middle Kingdom, the pharaohs built many new temples. Before construction began, a special ceremony called the "Stretching of the Cord" had to take place. Janet Van Duyn describes it in Egyptians: Pharaohs and Craftsmen.

"A priest held up his hand for silence. The chief architect of the temple picked up a coil of twine . . . and began to unwind it. He paced from stake to stake, tying the cord carefully at each angle, marking out the floor plan of the building. Here the great hall; here the sanctuary; here a courtyard.

A scribe was reading from an inscription on a stele, or large slab, to be placed in the temple courtyard commemorating the event. He praised His Majesty's efforts and concluded, 'Never has happened the like from the beginning.'

Surveyors following the . . . lines now drew markers in the sand with picks, indicating where trenches were to be dug. Then priests took over. Wearing their ceremonial leopard skins, they walked through the squared-off areas of rooms and corridors, placing symbolic objects in small pits dug in various corners. Buried models of building tools, amulets, even food and wine would complete the dedication of the temple to the god."

of the flood in the season of harvest. . . .

Twice great is the king of his city: he is as it were a rock barring the blast in the time of tempest. [39]

They Were Called Hyksos

As the pharaohs of the 12th Dynasty built up the strength and the prosperity of Egypt, the country attracted the interest of foreigners. Egypt was for the most part geographically isolated, but the Egyptians themselves had spread tales of their civilization through trade and military expeditions, especially in the Near East. Over time, a steady stream of immigrants from that area moved into the northern Delta.

As long as powerful men like Sesostris III and Amenemhet III were on the throne, the pharaohs remained in control. During the 13th Dynasty, however, a series of weak kings caused the power of the pharaohs to dwindle. As in the past, the local rulers grew more independent, and Egypt once more became divided against itself. But this time the weakened country lay open to invading hordes from the east.

Foreign rule finished off the political unity rebuilt during the Middle Kingdom pharaohs and brought about the period's decline.

The Egyptians called the invaders Hyksos, a Greek word meaning "rulers of foreign lands." The foreigners may have been filtering into Egypt since the 12th Dynasty, growing more dominant in the area as the pharaohs' grip on the country weakened. Then, in 1674 B.C., a final surge of Hyksos invaded from the Near East. They thundered into the Delta villages with horse-drawn war chariots, each carrying an archer who wore body armor and used

Amenemhet III, portrayed here in a stone carving, was one of the 12th Dynasty pharaohs who restored peace and prosperity to Egypt.

bows, lances, and new types of bronze swords. The Egyptians did their best to turn back the Hyksos, but fighting on foot with copper and stone weapons, they were no match for the mounted enemy warriors with their advanced weapons. Egypt was soundly defeated.

Ruled by Foreigners

The Egyptians were stunned—for fifteen centuries, they had been masters of their land and now they were subject to a crude force of foreigners. One ancient Egyptian account describes their devastation:

> [There was a king of ours whose name was Tutimaios.] In his reign, for what cause I know not, a blast of God smote [struck] us; and unexpectedly, from the regions of the East, invaders of an obscure [little-known] race marched in confidence of victory against our land. By main force they easily seized it without striking a blow; and having overpowered the rulers of the land, they then burned our cities ruthlessly, razed [tore down] to the ground the temples of the gods, and treated all the natives with a cruel hostility, massacring some and leading into slavery the wives and children of others. . . . Their race as a whole was called Hyksos. [40]

After their victory, the Hyksos consolidated their control of the Delta and established a capital at the city of Avaris, south of the Delta near Memphis. They adopted many Egyptian customs and ruled as pharaohs of the 15th to 17th Dynasties, dominating primarily Lower Egypt for more than a century. In time, however, a new Egyptian dynasty—the 17th—from Thebes managed to gain control of Upper Egypt. These rulers maintained Egyptian civilization, gaining strength and biding their time.

Finally, a powerful Theban ruler named Kamose determined to retake the lost territory and unite Egypt. To achieve this, he had to march not only against the Hyksos, but also against Nubia, which had broken free of Egypt and allied itself with the conquerors. Around 1578 B.C., Kamose gathered his nobles to discuss his plans:

Kamose, whom Re had appointed as the real king and had granted him

power . . . spoke in his palace to the council of grandees [nobles]: "I should like to know what serves this strength of mine, when a chieftain is in Avaris and another in Cush [Kush], and I sit united with an Asiatic [the Hyksos ruler] and a Nubian [the king of Kush], each man in possession of his slice of Egypt, and I cannot pass by him as far as Memphis. . . . I will grapple with him and slit open his belly. My desire is to deliver Egypt and to smite [strike down] the Asiatics [Hyksos]."[41]

Using the technologies and tactics of their conquerors, Kamose and his troops defeated a large Hyksos force and captured several towns under enemy control. Through these actions, the Egyptians won back control of the Nile River and its trade. Kamose soon died, however, and it was his brother Ahmose, the next Theban king, who finally broke the power of the Hyksos completely. After many years of fighting, Ahmose captured the Hyksos capital, Avaris, and drove the surviving Hyksos all the way to Syria. Once he had freed Egypt of these foreigners, Ahmose united Egypt under the power of Thebes, which became the new capital.

Although the Hyksos had no marked effect on Egypt's civilization, they were important in that the Egyptians' hatred for the intruders triggered a revival of unity that caused them to rise up and drive their enemies out. And the struggle shaped Egypt's foreign policy for years to come. To prove the greatness of their civilization and to make up for the terrible blow to national pride that the Hyksos conquest had delivered, Egypt sought to expand its country into an empire. And they used their enemies' weapons to do it.

6 The New Kingdom: The Egyptian Empire

Ahmose had spent years campaigning against the Hyksos in Egypt and the Near East before they finally surrendered. During this time, his army, equipped with horse-drawn chariots and other weapons introduced by the Hyksos, had become a battle-hardened, efficient fighting force. When Ahmose became pharaoh, he kept the army intact so it was available to him at all times. No longer did the ruler have to depend on part-time soldiers provided by the nomarchs for emergencies.

With this army behind him—and with his own abilities as a leader—Ahmose established his control over all of Egypt and founded the 18th Dynasty. This new dynasty ushered in a period known as the New Kingdom, which lasted from 1552 to 1069 B.C. During these years, Ahmose and his successors, with the memory of the Hyksos invasion still burning in their minds, created a vast empire that completely dominated the Near East.

The Beginnings of an Empire

Once he had driven the invaders out, Ahmose had to rebuild the nation, which was emerging from two hundred years of turmoil. To help carry the burden of an ex-panding government, Ahmose appointed two viziers instead of one. He also divided the land into new administrative districts and created a vast army of officials to handle local government in each. Their chief loyalty was to the pharaoh.

The reins of power were thus kept out of the hands of the powerful local nobles, many of whom were descendants of the great Middle Kingdom nomarchs and had fought not only the Hyksos, but Ahmose as well. Besides depriving them of their political power by appointing new government officials, Ahmose also seized their lands. Once again, most of Egypt was part of the pharaoh's estate. As a result, the old landed nobility, who had formed the backbone of government during the Middle Kingdom, just about disappeared.

As the number of officials grew, so did the job opportunities of Egypt's middle class. One official described how he became a supervisor of the production of gold statues of the gods:

> I was one whose family was poor and whose town was small, but the Lord of the Two Lands [pharaoh] recognized me; I was accounted great in his heart, and the king in his role as sun-god in the splendour of his palace saw me. He exalted [set above] me more than

The Great Empire Builder

As Thutmose III grew older, his hatred of Hatshepsut increased. But he bided his time and secured the support of the powerful priests of Amen-Re at Karnak, with whom he was living. Then, one day in 1458 B.C., Hatshepsut suddenly—and mysteriously—died, and Thutmose III took his rightful place on the throne. Some speculated that Thutmose, with the priests as his allies, had her poisoned.

Once Thutmose III was pharaoh, he set out on a campaign of conquest greater than Egypt had ever seen. During Hatshepsut's reign, little control was exerted over the city-states in Palestine and Syria that had been conquered by earlier pharaohs. As a result, many of these areas had not seen an Egyptian army in the twenty-one years Hatshepsut had ruled. They desperately wanted their freedom from Egypt and its required tribute. They decided now was the time to revolt.

Determined to regain control of city-states, Thutmose III assembled a huge, twenty-thousand-man army at the northeastern border of Egypt. It was the largest in ancient Egyptian history and was led by the pharaoh himself, in a gold and silver war chariot. For this was the age of empire and, unlike earlier times, the rulers were generals, too.

Thutmose led his army to Megiddo, a city south of modern-day Haifa in Israel. The pharaoh and his soldiers were met outside Megiddo's walls by the forces of three hundred city-state princes, ready to fight for freedom from Egyptian rule. When the battle was over, Thutmose and his troops had won, and the tribute and taxes from the reconquered city-states

added to Egypt's wealth. To discourage the defeated rebels from attempting to revolt again, the pharaoh ordered his soldiers to sever one hand from each dead enemy who had fallen in battle.

By the end of his reign, Thutmose III had extended the boundaries of Egypt north to the Euphrates River at the border of Mesopotamia and south to the fourth cataract of the Nile in what is today northern Sudan. Battle hymns to Thutmose III were written. In one, the god Amen-Re talked to Thutmose:

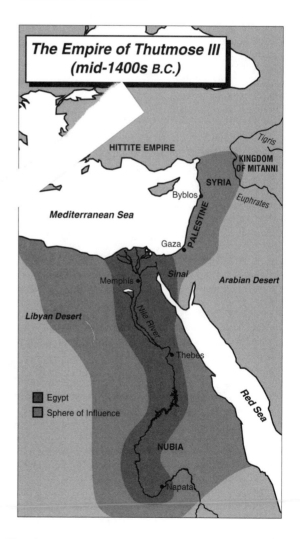

The Empire of Thutmose III (mid-1400s B.C.)

HITTITE EMPIRE

Tigris

KINGDOM OF MITANNI

SYRIA

Byblos

Euphrates

Mediterranean Sea

PALESTINE

Gaza

Memphis

Sinai

Arabian Desert

Libyan Desert

Nile River

Thebes

Red Sea

■ Egypt
□ Sphere of Influence

NUBIA

Napata

Give Breath to Us

After the initial victory at Megiddo, Thutmose III and his soldiers settled down to a long siege of the city. Finally, the princes came out and begged for mercy. Their plea is quoted in When Egypt Ruled the East *by George Steindorff and Keith C. Seele.*

"Then that fallen one [the chief of Kadesh], together with the chiefs who were with him, caused all their children to come forth to my majesty with many products of gold and silver, all their horses and all their trappings, their great chariots of gold and silver with their painted equipment, all their battle armor, their bows, their arrows, and all their implements [tools] of war—those things, indeed, with which they had come to fight against my majesty. And now they brought them as tribute to my majesty while they stood on their walls giving praise to my majesty in order that the breath of life might be given to them.

Then my majesty caused them to swear an oath, saying 'Never again will we do evil against Menkheperre [Thutmose III]—may he live forever—our lord, in our lifetime, for we have witnessed his power. Let him only give breath to us according to his desire.'"

A relief found in Thutmose III's temple depicts Thutmose slaying his enemies.

I have come, giving thee to smite [wipe out] the princes of Zahi [western Syria], I have hurled them beneath thy feet among their highlands. . . . Thou hast trampled those who are in the districts of Punt. . . . I have made them see thy majesty as a circling star. . . . Crete and Cyprus are in terror. . . . Those who are in the midst of the great sea hear thy roarings; I have made them see thy majesty as an avenger, rising upon the back of his slain victim. . . . I have made them see thy majesty as a fierce-eyed lion, while thou makest them corpses in their valleys. [44]

After conquering these lands, Thutmose III stationed a skeleton force of soldiers and officials in each state, most of which were nonetheless allowed to govern themselves. However, they were required to be subordinate to Egypt and owed their loyalty to the pharaoh, to whom they paid tribute.

Egypt now became wealthier than ever before as tribute from the conquered states in the Near East and Nubia poured into the country, riches that included silver, gold, lapis lazuli, turquoise, ivory, myrrh (a substance from certain trees used to make perfume), cinnamon wood, ebony, monkeys, hunting dogs, leopard skins, and incense. In addition to claiming material goods, Egypt also enslaved conquered peoples to provide the labor to build beautiful new temples and tombs.

The Rebel Pharaoh

For a time, the Egyptian empire flourished. However, about 1350 B.C. Amen-

Amenhotep IV created a religious uproar when he revealed his belief in one supreme god.

hotep IV took the throne and created a serious religious crisis that critically damaged the empire. The new pharaoh had been influenced by some radical Egyptian priests, who were exploring the possibility that a single mighty god controlled everything, including the other gods. Some scholars believe this to be the beginning of the idea of a universal creator.

In time, Amenhotep came to believe that the supreme god was Aten, which was the physical sun itself, rather than the sun god, Re. He even composed a hymn to the new god:

Thou art in my heart,

There is no other that knoweth thee,

Save thy son Ikhnaton [Akhenaten].

Thou hast made him wise in thy
designs

And in thy might.

The world is in thy hand,

Even as thou hast made them.

When thou hast risen, they live;

When thou settest they die.

When thou risest, they are made to
     grow . . . for the king.

Since thou did establish the earth,

Thou hast raised them up for thy son,

Who came forth from thy limbs,

The lord of the Two Lands.[45]

As pharaoh, Amenhotep IV decided to use his power to change the Egyptian religion and make Aten the god of the empire. He closed the temples of the principal god, Amen-Re, including Karnak, and broke up the priesthood. All the temples' lands and goods were turned over to the crown. The pharaoh changed his name from Amenhotep, meaning "Amen Is Satisfied," to Akhenaten, meaning "He Who Is Beneficial to Aten." Then he announced to the stunned people of Thebes that he was leaving their city and moving to a great new city to be built in the desert called Akhetaten, or "Horizon of Aten." To Akhetaten, Thebes was still the city of Amen-Re. Before long, the once-thriving capital was nearly deserted. Weeds grew in Karnak.

Accompanying Akhenaten to his new city in the desert was his Great Royal Wife, Nefertiti. Along with his mother, Tiy, she shared Akhenaten's dream of one god, and both influenced the pharaoh greatly. Married to Amenhotep as a teenager, the beautiful Nefertiti was widely loved and admired. One monument that archaeolo-

Akhenaten's Great Royal Wife Nefertiti (pictured) had a profound influence on her husband's belief in a single god.

gists have since dug up out of the sands said that she was "mistress of loveliness; great in popularity; the woman whose being gladdens the lord of both lands [Upper and Lower Egypt]."[46]

Akhenaten believed in realism and introduced it as a new concept in art; surviving works more closely resemble art of the modern day than the idealistic portrayals of the Old Kingdom. The pharaoh urged the artists of his capital to present their subjects as they really looked—wrinkles, warts, and all. Akhenaten even had himself portrayed with his unflatteringly long jaw and rounded stomach.

Akhenaten and Nefertiti lived in peace in the pharaoh's dream city for only a few years. The priests of Amen-Re hated the pharaoh for depriving them of their livelihood and power. Behind the scenes, they worked against him at every turn. They had plenty of opportunity, since at the same time, the empire was in trouble.

Akhenaten was so preoccupied with his new religion that he took no action

The Little Queen-to-Be

As Akhenaten's future queen, Nefertiti had luxurious rooms in the royal palace. Already the people of the court had started to gather there, hoping to gain the favor of the little queen-to-be. Evelyn Wells describes the future queen's rooms in her biography Nefertiti.

"As for Nefertiti, she opened her eyes in a bed carved and painted and gilded by one of the great Theban artists, with pillow and mattress of the softest goat's wool. . . . The bed sheets were of the softest, silkiest, hand-woven linen, and her . . . cheek rested on a crescent-shaped headrest . . . of carved and painted wood or colored glass. . . .

Hanging on the painted walls or spread on the floors were rich tapestries and finely woven mats. Others hung on the windows to keep out the heat of the sun or the sand from the desert when the wind blew. There were many tables, small and large, and beautiful little . . . footstools and chairs. . . . There was furniture of rare cedar brought from Lebanon, and ebony overlaid with ivory on gold leaf, or studded with gold, made . . . without nails, but studded as fine furniture would be, centuries later, in Europe. . . .

On every gleaming surface were set large, handsome lamps, and vases filled with flowers, and colored glass bowls where bright, live fish swam. And scattered everywhere were the small, exquisite bibelots [trinkets] Egyptians cherished . . . such as tiny statuettes of the gods and the divine animals, in wood . . . pottery, alabaster, silver, or gold. . . . There were goblets and small . . . vases and bottles and jars and bowls of every possible size and kind [which were often] . . . crusted with jewels.

Many of these would be presents given her by Akhenaton. Every Egyptian lavished all the gifts he could afford on the girl he was to marry."

Save Me from Monsters

By the New Kingdom, Egyptians believed the dead went beneath Egypt to the Underworld, where Osiris ruled. Once there, the deceased faced many trials, including horrible monsters. In Spell 17 of the Book of the Dead, *quoted in Eric Hornung's* The Valley of the Kings, *the deceased begs the gods for mercy.*

"Save me from that dog-faced god
Whose eyebrows are human,
Who lives off the victims of war,
Guarding the meanders [winding paths] of the Lake of
     Fire,
Swallowing corpses and dominating hearts,
Wounding without being seen . . .
Seizing souls and lapping up rot,
Living from the putrid [rotten];
The guardian of darkness in obscurity [hiding]
Terrorizing the weary.
Their knives shall not pierce me
And down to their slaughterhouses I shall not go,
To their butcher's blocks
To abide their traps.
Nothing shall be prepared for me from that which the
gods detest."

Osiris, ruler of the Underworld, as portrayed in an ancient Egyptian wall painting.

The solid gold coffin that contained the mummy of the 18th Dynasty pharaoh Tutankhamen. With Tutankhamen's rule, Amen-Re was once again worshiped as the principal god.

pharaoh. He was just a boy, only ten or eleven years old. But under the guidance of Ay, a high court official, he wiped out the new religion and brought the country back to Amen-Re. The young pharaoh changed his name to Tutankhamen in the god's honor and moved his court back to Thebes, leaving behind an empty, desolate city that was soon covered by the eternal sands of Egypt. Tutankhamen restored both the priesthood and the temples of the old god. The memory of the rebel pharaoh was wiped out. It was against the law even to mention his name. After ruling only a short time, Tutankhamen died, and soon the once-brilliant 18th Dynasty came to a close.

Only a Moment of Glory

Around 1295 B.C., Ramses I, who had served as vizier under the pharaoh Horemheb, founded the 19th Dynasty. The new ruler came from a long line of soldiers. He held the throne only briefly, but his son and grandson—Seti I and Ramses II—like Thutmose III, were great warrior-pharaohs. They were determined to recapture for Egypt the empire in the Near East that Akhenaten had lost. They dreamed of restoring Egypt to its former glory. And they did—for only a moment in time.

Ramses II, who was the greatest pharaoh of the 19th Dynasty, faced a dangerous situation in Syria. His father, Seti I, had reconquered Palestine and southern Syria to the city of Kadesh. But Seti had not been able to reclaim northern Syria from the Hittites, a conquering people who had seized the land from Egypt. Now, the Hittites had put together a great army,

when enemies such as the Hittites invaded Egypt's northern Syrian territories. Loyal princes wrote the pharaoh, begging for his help. One nearly despaired, saying "thy city [Tunip] weeps, and her tears are flowing and there is no help for us."[47] But the pharaoh refused to send aid. As a result, Egypt lost most of its lands in the Near East, reducing the size of its empire.

To maintain its empire, Egypt needed more than an original thinker, which Akhenaten surely was. It needed a pharaoh who was a strong, practical ruler, as well as a skilled military leader. The historian E. A. Wallis Budge says of Akhenaten that "he failed to see that only a warrior could hold what warriors had won."[48] When Akhenaten died, his dream—and the city in the desert—died with him.

Within a short time after Akhenaten's death, his son-in-law, Tutankhaten, became

Determined to restore Egypt to its former glory, Seti I and Ramses II regained some of the empire in the Near East during their reigns. The great warrior Seti I (left) stands before gods Horus and Osiris in this relief in his temple. Seti's son, Ramses II (below), battles with the Hittites in an attempt to gain northern Syria.

which was assembled at Kadesh. Determined to finish what his father had started and oust the Hittites, Ramses II met them at Kadesh about 1275 B.C.

Unaware of the exact position of his enemy, Ramses had moved ahead of his army with a few troops when the Hittites attacked. His troops, far outnumbered, fled. But without hesitating, Ramses "drove at a gallop and charged the forces of the Foe from Hatti [the Hittites], being alone by himself, none other with him."[49] Surrounded by twenty-five hundred chariots, the pharaoh called on Amen for help and, according to legend, hacked at the enemy for three long hours until the Egyptian army arrived. Ramses and the Egyptians claimed a great victory, but the Hittites claimed Egypt had retreated and that they had won.

Regardless of who won that particular battle, conflict between the two peoples continued for years, until Ramses II and Hattusilis III, the next Hittite ruler, finally ended it with the first peace treaty be-

A nineteenth-century illustration of the colossal statues of Ramses II that cut into the cliffs at Abu Simbel. Similar statues of Ramses II appeared throughout Egypt as symbols of the great pharaoh's power.

tween two nations in recorded history. Although Ramses II did not recover all of the lands won by Thutmose III, he regained Palestine and part of Syria.

A Lengthy Reign

The peace brought about by this treaty allowed Ramses to turn his attention homeward, and he returned to his new capital at Tanis in the northeastern Delta. His reign lasted an astonishing sixty-seven years and was the longest known in ancient Egypt. The average life span at the time was only twenty to thirty years; Ramses lived to about ninety. He outlived his beloved Queen Nefertari and many of his more than one hundred children. His thirteenth son, Merneptah, was over sixty when he took the throne in 1212 B.C.

On the surface, Egypt seemed more prosperous and stable than ever. Ahmose had driven the hated foreigners out of the kingdom and founded the 18th Dynasty.

His successors restored the absolute power of the pharaohs and carved out an empire for Egypt in the Near East and Nubia. Seti I and Ramses II managed to recapture some of the lands that had been lost as a result of Akhenaten's religious revolution.

The vast riches that poured into Egypt as a result of foreign conquest had made the land of the pharaohs even more powerful and had triggered a burst of cultural activity. With the wealth gained from tribute, for example, Ramses II built so many monuments in Egypt that one ancient source said, "He has made his monuments like the stars of the heavens." [50]

Statues of the great pharaoh covered the land. Some of the most famous are the four giant, seated statues of Ramses II at the temple at Abu Simbel north of Wadi Halfa in present-day northern Sudan. These drew worldwide attention when they were dismantled and moved prior to the building of the Aswan Dam between 1964 and 1968. Over $40 million was spent to save them from the rising water

Forward, I Am with You

At Kadesh, Ramses II found himself alone surrounded by the enemy. He cried out to Amen for help. His cry, quoted in Nicholas Grimal's A History of Ancient Egypt, *was heard and with new strength flowing through him, the pharaoh hacked his way to freedom.*

"I call to you my father Amun [Amen],
I am among a host of strangers;
All countries are arrayed [stand together] against me,
I am alone, there's none with me.
My numerous troops have deserted me,
I keep on shouting for them,
But none of them heeds my call.
I know Amun helps me more than a million troops,
More than a hundred thousand charioteers,
More than ten thousand brothers and sons
Who are united as one heart . . .
Now though I prayed in the distant land . . .
I found Amun came when I called to him,
He gave me his hand and I rejoiced.
He called from behind as if nearby:
'Forward, I am with you.'"

of Lake Nasser. Many nations took part in this rescue operation.

The New Kingdom was also known for its temples, and the many slaves captured in battle provided the labor to build them. Smaller temples had carved stone columns that formed a portico (porch) surrounding an inner court. In larger temples, like that of Amen-Re at Karnak, the columns were within the temple walls in a huge hypostyle hall, or hall of pillars.

These pillars supported the flat roof. Outside Karnak and other temples, the pharaohs raised huge stone obelisks—tall, thin pillars with pyramid points at the top—on which they carved accounts of their achievements.

Despite these advances in politics, commerce, and culture, the foundation of the Egyptian empire had been cracked by Akhenaten's religious revolution, and the crack was about to grow wider.

Chapter

7 The Decline of Ancient Egypt

When Ramses II died, the Egyptian empire had been a powerful force for more than three hundred years. The 18th Dynasty warrior-pharaohs had aggressively conquered other lands. The spirit of conquest continued under Seti I and Ramses II, even though they were retaking lands that had once already belonged to Egypt. However, after Ramses II's death the long, slow decline of Egypt began. His successors steadily lost control of the country, destroying the unity and power regained by earlier New Kingdom rulers. Egypt's pharaohs also went on the defensive, struggling to preserve, rather than to extend, the empire. Except for a few brief attempts to restore it, Egypt's days as the greatest power of the ancient world were over.

Just a Figurehead

Egypt fell because of conditions within its borders. In time, the pharaoh became more of a figurehead. There were two reasons for this. First, most of the rulers who followed Ramses II were weak and could not manage either the empire or Egypt's domestic affairs.

Second, over time the Egyptians' view of their ruler had changed. When Egypt

Egypt's glory days in the ancient world ended with the death of Ramses II (pictured), after which the country fell into a slow decline.

broke out of its isolation and conquered other nations, the pharaoh began interacting with other countries and their rulers. In communicating directly with them, whether leading his troops into battle or arranging a peace treaty, he was behaving more like an ordinary human than an unapproachable divine ruler. He was a king among kings instead of the remote and mysterious being of earlier times. As a result, although the pharaoh was still officially worshiped as a god, he was neither respected nor feared as he once had been.

As had happened before in Egypt's history when the pharaohs were weak, the priests gained more power. The rulers after Ramses II had continued the policy of giving wealth, including land, to the temples—especially the temples of Amen-Re—to ensure the favor of the gods. Soon, the temples controlled nearly 15 percent of the country—750,000 acres—and the people who lived on those acres. The people were included because the peasants who worked the land were still serfs. So, when the pharaoh gave away a piece of property, they went with it. At one time, the temples owned not only agricultural lands, but also 169 towns in Egypt, Syria, and Kush. They even had their own ships.

Ramses III described some of the many gifts he had bestowed on the temples of Amen-Re:

> I filled its [Amen-Re's] treasury with the products of the land of Egypt: gold, silver, every costly stone by the hundred thousand. Its granary was overflowing with barley and wheat; its lands, its herds, their multitudes were like the sand of the shore. I taxed for it the Southland [Upper Egypt] as well as the Northland [Lower Egypt]; Nu-bia and Syria came to it, bearing their impost [tribute]. It was filled with captives, which thou gavest me among the Nine Bows [foreigners]. . . . I multiplied these divine offerings presented before thee, of bread, wine, beer, and fat geese; numerous oxen, bullocks [young bulls], calves, cows, white oryxes [antelopes], and gazelles offered in his slaughter yard.[51]

The temples were gaining not only economic but political power. By the time Ramses XI, the last pharaoh of the New Kingdom, came to power, the high priest of Amen-Re at Karnak was no longer selected by the pharaoh. Instead, the position had become hereditary and was now

As a peace offering to the gods, Ramses III (pictured) lavished the temples with gifts, lessening his own power and strengthening the power of the priests.

passed from father to son. The position became so powerful that no pharaoh could rule without the goodwill of the high priest. In time, this official would even usurp, or illegally seize, the throne.

As in the time of the Middle Kingdom, the pharaoh's income was shrinking because he continued to give away land to the gods but no longer replenished his coffers with new conquests. The pharaoh could no longer meet his commitments to feed workers, such as the tomb builders who labored in his service in the Valley of the Kings. Because the valley was so barren, the pharaoh had to provide them with any and all supplies. Receiving none, the workers actually staged the first strike ever recorded. When asked why, one man said, "It is because of hunger and thirst."[52]

The fact that in the tombs nearby the dead glittered with gold and jewels while they went unpaid made many workers angry. As a result, they helped robbers plunder the tombs in the Valley of the Kings and traded their share of the riches for food. As the pharaoh's control weakened, tomb robbers grew ever more daring. By the reign of Ramses IX, the royal tombs in the Valley of the Kings were being looted systematically by an organized gang. One of its members was beaten with a stick until he confessed, saying, "We collected the gold which we found on this noble mummy of this god . . . and on the coffins in which he lay."[53]

Unrest outside Egypt also contributed to its decline. New enemies from the Near East, Greece, and Italy, who had been pushed out of their lands by invaders from farther north, were on the move. They were called the Sea Peoples by the Egyptians because they were from the Mediterranean area. Searching for new homes and riches, their warriors set out, followed by baggage wagons, cattle, women, and children—and their fleet. They rolled through Syria and Palestine, crushing the Hittites and threatening Egypt.

In 1178 B.C., Ramses III roused the nation and defeated the Sea Peoples. Afterwards, the pharaoh said, "As for those who reached my boundary . . . their souls are finished unto all eternity."[54] The Egyptians had joined together and saved their home. But they were defending their boundaries—not fighting on foreign soil to win lands for the empire as Thutmose III had fought at Megiddo or Ramses II had at Kadesh. Before long, the Sea Peoples had taken over Egypt's last holdings in Palestine. By the time Ramses XI was on the throne, Nubia was the only foreign territory that remained under Egypt's control. Soon it, too, broke free. The Egyptian empire was at an end.

Egypt Splits in Two

At the end of the New Kingdom, Egypt entered a period of confusion and unrest worse than any it had ever experienced. Egypt once more split into two lands and had two pharaohs. Around 1069 B.C., after the death of Ramses XI, a noble called Smendes conquered the Delta and claimed the throne. He and his successors in the new 21st Dynasty ruled Lower Egypt from Tanis. Upper Egypt was governed from Thebes, the traditional New Kingdom capital, by Herihor, high priest of Amen-Re, and his successors. From this point on, Egypt remained divided much of the time. In fact, the land was so divided politically that rival dynasties often overlapped.

The decline of the pharaohs ruined Egypt's prestige with other countries, especially in the Near East, a good deal of which it had once ruled. One summer, Wenamon, a government official, set out from Thebes. Upper Egypt's ruler, Herihor, had decided to send him as his representative to Byblos, to buy wood to build a sacred boat for Amen-Re.

Unlike representatives of the all-powerful pharaohs of earlier times, Wenamon had no ships and very little gold and silver for payment. Since he had to pass through the territory ruled by Smendes, Wenamon sought an audience with him to get his permission to leave the country and to get help booking passage on a ship. On board, what little money he had was stolen.

Upon arriving in Byblos, Wenamon tried to see the prince, who refused to see him. Finally, after nearly a month, the prince called Wenamon into his presence. Angered, Wenamon tried to use the authority of the pharaoh to get the wood, saying, "Your father supplied it, your grandfather did so, and you too shall do it."[55]

But the ruler of Byblos, who had once bowed down to Egypt, was not moved. Wenamon was trading on the memory of Egypt's former greatness. And the prince did not have to turn over the wood for nothing to the representative of a weak ruler of a declining, divided nation. The prince made his position clear, saying:

Where is the fine ship which Nesubenebded [Smendes] would have

Stealing from the Dead

As the Old Kingdom began to disintegrate, Egyptians began robbing the tombs of their pharaohs. During periods of great unrest and weak rulers, these incidents increased. As quoted in Morris Brierbrier's The Tomb-Builders of the Pharaohs, *one of these thieves recounts his gang's deeds.*

"We opened their outer coffins and their inner coffins in which they lay. We found the noble mummy of this king equipped with a sword. A large number of amulets and ornaments of gold were upon his neck. His mask of gold was upon him. The noble mummy of the king was completely covered with gold. His coffins were adorned with gold and silver inside and out and inlaid with all kinds of precious stones. We collected the gold which we found on this noble mummy of this god and on his amulets and jewels which were upon his neck and on the coffins in which he lay. We found the queen in exactly the same state and we collected all that we found on her likewise. We set fire to their coffins. We stole their furniture that we found with them consisting of articles of gold, silver, and bronze and divided them up amongst ourselves."

Ramses III holds back an invasion by the Libyans in a relief from the temple of Ramses III.

given you, and where is its picked Syrian crew? He would not put you and your affairs in charge of this skipper of yours, who might have had you killed and thrown into the sea. . . . I am neither your servant nor the servant of him who sent you here. If I cry out to Lebanon the heavens open and the logs lie here on the shore of the sea. [56]

At this point, Wenamon appealed to Amen-Re and promised to return to Tanis to get goods to trade for the cedar. Finally, the prince reluctantly agreed to load the wood. Thutmose III or Ramses II would have been able to demand the wood and would have backed up that demand with troops.

Wolves at the Door

Conditions at home made Egypt an easy target for conquest by the states around it.

The Libyans were the first to attempt it. They gained the throne of the pharaohs without even drawing a sword. The Libyans had been filtering into the rich Delta from their more barren lands to the west since prehistoric times. Both Merneptah and Ramses III had beaten back actual invasions, but the immigration continued.

Most Libyans who settled in Egypt had adopted Egyptian customs. Their soldiers played an important role in the army of the pharaohs under the empire, who had depended on foreign mercenaries to build up their forces. In time, Libyan commanders were put in control of key Delta towns and soon gained positions of power in government.

One of these commanders, Shoshenq, was in control of Herakleopolis in Upper Egypt, which had been settled by his ancestors. The area he controlled now extended north to Memphis and south to Asyut. When the 21st Dynasty came to an end around 945 B.C., Shoshenq moved to

A relief image depicts Shoshenq I holding prisoners by their long hair. A Libyan commander, Shoshenq became an Egyptian pharaoh and conquered Upper Egypt and Thebes, briefly creating a unified Egypt.

Bubastis, a city in the eastern Delta, and proclaimed himself pharaoh. The fact that a foreign soldier was now ruler of Egypt was a direct result of the policy of conquest under the empire when the army became all-important.

Shoshenq I briefly united Egypt by conquering Upper Egypt, including Thebes, and using his power to have his son named high priest of Amen-Re, which was still a key position. The new pharaoh then renewed the long-dead drive for empire, recapturing lands in Palestine and Syria all the way to the city of Megiddo. Shoshenq I's gains were only temporary, however. Egypt was just too far gone for him to revive it. The weaker pharaohs who followed Shoshenq lost control, and much of the land broke up into the small feudal states from which it had arisen.

With the control of the Libyan pharaohs disintegrating, the land of the pharaohs was ripe for invasion. And the Kushites were glad to oblige. During the New Kingdom, Egypt had conquered Kush, or Lower Nubia, in present-day northern Sudan, and it had remained part of the Egyptian empire for nearly five hundred years before it won back its independence. But in 760 B.C., the Kushite king, Kashta, set out to conquer Egypt and won some territory.

By 722 B.C., his son Piankhy controlled Upper Egypt as far as Herakleopolis. The invasion of the Kushites rallied some of the Egyptians. Prince Tefnakht of Sais, a city in the western Delta, conquered Lower Egypt and marched south to stop Piankhy. But Piankhy launched his own invasion and defeated this force, taking the rest of Egypt. As a result, Piankhy and the other Kushite pharaohs ruled Egypt for the next seventy years as the 25th Dynasty. Like the Libyans, however, they ruled as though they were Egyptian pharaohs. Kush had been a part of Egypt for so long that the Kushites had adopted Egyptian customs.

Meanwhile, another potential conqueror, the kingdom of Assyria, was rising to power in the Near East. Unlike the Libyans and the Kushites, the Assyrians had absolutely no regard for Egyptian customs. And they were known far and wide for their cruelty to those they defeated. One Assyrian king described what he did to his enemies:

> I built a pillar over against the city gate, and I flayed [took the skin off] all the chief men who had revolted, and I covered the pillar with their skins; some I walled up within the pillar, some I impaled upon the pillar on stakes [drove a stake through them and into the pillar, leaving the body hanging in midair], and others I bound to stakes round about the pillar. . . . Many captives among them I burned with fire. . . . From some I cut off their hands and their fingers, and from others I cut off their noses, their ears, and their fingers, of many I put out the eyes. I made one pillar of the living and another of heads, and I bound their heads to tree trunks round about the city. [57]

In 670 B.C., the Assyrians attacked Egypt. They defeated Piankhy's son, Taharka, and conquered Lower Egypt. Because of conquests under the empire and the trade that had since opened up, this area had now become more important

---

One Step Forward, Two Steps Back

After Piankhy defeated the Egyptian Tefnakht, who had taken the field against him, he conquered the rest of Egypt city by city. Tefnakht, who had escaped to the Delta, sent a letter to Piankhy seeking a truce; it is quoted in Nicholas Grimal's A History of Ancient Egypt.

"While I am under just reproach, you did not smite me in accordance with my crime. Weigh in the balance . . . and multiply it against me threefold! (But) leave the seed, that you may gather it in time [do not kill me]. Do not cut down the grove to its roots! Have mercy! Dread of you is in my body: fear of you is in my bones!

I sit not at the beer feast; the harp is not brought for me. I eat the bread of the hungry; I drink the water of the thirsty, since the day you heard my name! Illness is in my bones, my head is bald, my clothes are rags. . . . Let my goods be received into the treasury: gold and all precious stones, the best of the horses, and payment of every kind. Send me a messenger quickly, to drive the fear from my heart."

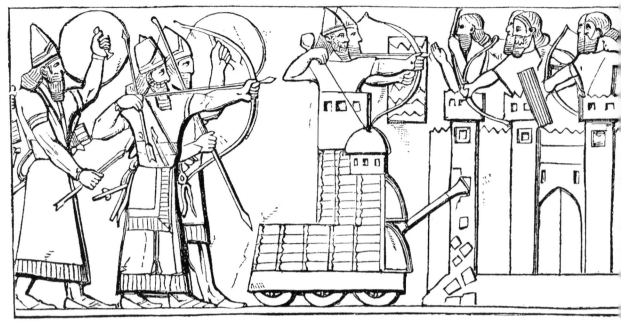

Assyrians use a battering ram to attack their enemy. Their brutal attack on Egypt left the country devastated.

than Upper Egypt. The Assyrians made the Delta lords take an oath of loyalty as vassals of their empire. They put one of them, Necho I of Sais, in charge of the country. But then the Assyrians returned home. The rumble of revolt began as soon as they left, and Necho was a ringleader.

The Assyrians had to come back to Egypt twice to reassert their dominance. By the second time, they were furious. They took the Delta and pursued the fleeing Kushite ruler through Upper Egypt, driving him back to his homeland. On the way, they sacked Thebes, the great religious center of Egypt. The Assyrian ruler boasted of his success, "Heavy booty, beyond counting, I took away from Thebes. Against Egypt and Cush [Kush] I let my weapons rage and showed my might."[58] At the end of their bloody conquest, Assyria announced to the world that Egypt's greatness was in the past.

The Last Egyptian Pharaohs

While the Assyrians were busy fighting a war elsewhere, a new line of pharaohs came along who briefly restored some of Egypt's greatness. These rulers managed to create one bright moment in the long darkness of decline, but it was the last gasp of a dying nation. Around 663 B.C., Necho's son, Psammetichus I, proclaimed himself pharaoh and founded the 26th Dynasty.

Psammetichus I was one of the ablest rulers ever to sit on the throne of Egypt. Like Amenemhet I of the Middle Kingdom, he broke the power of the Delta lords who had been causing trouble for so long. Then, Psammetichus I attempted to re-establish the Egypt of the past, to revive its former strength by bringing back the art, architecture, literature, and religion of the Old Kingdom. For this reason, historians have called this period the Restoration. But the pharaohs could not bring back the past. It was too late.

Backed by an army filled with Greek mercenaries, Psammetichus I regained control over Upper Egypt. The pharaoh established new trading connections, especially with Greece. Foreign merchants, as well as foreign soldiers, contributed to the prosperity of Egypt during this time. Business was once more booming, especially trade with Greece. Much of this wealth from trade went toward supporting the army, for Psammetichus I knew that without this army Egypt was lost.

Necho II, Psammetichus's successor, not only continued to foster trade, but also moved to rebuild Egypt's ancient empire. He marched northward to take back Egypt's former holdings in Syria and Palestine. In the end, however, he was defeated, crushed by Nebuchadrezzar, king of Babylonia, the nation that had displaced Assyria as the great power in the Near East.

Sais, a City to be Respected

One Egyptian official, Udjahorresnet, gave advice to the Persian king, Cambyses, so he could act like a real Egyptian pharaoh. All that he asked in return was that the Persians treat his native city, Sais, with respect as the home of Neith, mother of the great god Re. In Nicholas Grimal's A History of Ancient Egypt, Udjahorresnet describes what happened.

"I let His Majesty know that greatness of Sais, that it is the seat of Neith-the-Great, the mother who bore Ra [Re]. . . . I made a petition of the majesty of the King of Upper and Lower Egypt, Cambyses, about all the foreigners who dwelled in the temple of Neith, in order to have them expelled from it, so as to let the temple of Neith be in all its splendour, as it has been before. His Majesty commanded to expel all the foreigners who dwelled in the temple of Neith, to demolish all their houses and all their unclean things that were in this temple.

When they had carried all their personal belongings outside the wall of the temple, His Majesty commanded to cleanse the temple of Neith and to return all its personnel to it. . . . His Majesty commanded to give divine offerings to Neith-the-Great, the mother of god, and to the great gods of Sais. . . . His Majesty commanded to perform all their festivals and all their possessions. . . . His Majesty did this because I had let [him] know the greatness of Sais, that it is the city of all the gods, who dwell there on their seats forever."

Babylonian king Nebuchadrezzar forced the Egyptians out of the Near East, sending Egypt into its final decline.

Nebuchadrezzar drove the Egyptians out of the Near East and followed their retreating army all the way to the border of Egypt. At this point, however, Necho's forces turned and, like the troops under Ramses III, successfully defended the borders of their land. A biblical account describes how Nebuchadrezzar had devastated Egypt's power:

> The king of Egypt came not again any more out of his land; for the king of Babylon had taken, from the brook of Egypt unto the river Euphrates, all that pertained to the king of Egypt.[59]

The Saite Period of Egyptian rule came to an end when a new power in the Near East, Persia, stormed Egypt's borders in 525 B.C. After the invasion, the Persians ruled for a little over a century as the 27th Dynasty, and Egypt became a satrap, or province, of the Persian Empire. During the 400s B.C., the Egyptians revolted several times and finally threw off the Persian yoke.

For the next almost sixty years, the last native Egyptian pharaohs ruled their homeland. To the Persians, however, Egypt was just a rebellious province that had managed to gain its independence temporarily. In 343 B.C., the great Artaxerxes put down the rebellion for good. Realizing that the cause was lost, Nectanebo II, the last pharaoh of the 30th Dynasty, fled to the south into Kush. Once he left his throne, Egypt, land of the pharaohs, passed into history.

Just eleven years later, in 332 B.C., the Greeks under Alexander the Great conquered the Persian Empire and Egypt along with it. For the next three hundred or so years, the Greeks ruled as pharaohs in Egypt. But in 30 B.C., the country became part of the Roman Empire, and the last Greek ruler, Cleopatra, committed suicide rather than be led in triumph to Rome. With the coming of the Romans and Christianity, Egyptian culture, which had endured through thousands of years and many invasions, started to fade away. By the time the Arabs and Islam conquered the country in A.D. 640, ancient Egyptian civilization seemed to have disappeared—or had it?

8 The Legacy of the Ancient Egyptians

The era of Egypt's greatness had come to a close. But the land of the pharaohs left later civilizations a precious legacy. The Egyptians were pioneers in astronomy, mathematics, art, architecture, medicine, writing, and literature. They were giants, far ahead of other civilizations in their thinking. As Jean-Francois Champollion states, "The Egyptians of old thought like men a hundred feet tall."[60]

The Egyptians passed many of these achievements on to other peoples, playing a significant part in the development of world civilization. Both trade and expansion brought other peoples into contact with Egyptian culture, which influenced Syria and Palestine to the east, along with Nubia and Kush to the south. Egyptian civilization also made an impact on Egypt's conquerors, the Greeks and the Romans, who in turn spread their knowledge to western Europe.

"The Greatest Symphonies"

The ancient Greeks counted the Great Pyramid of Khufu at Giza as one of the Seven Wonders of the World, and it is the only one still standing. Scholar Jean Capart has called it the "mightiest architectural effort of the human race."[61] One modern-day author described what he felt when he saw it:

> The Great Pyramid of Cheops [Khufu]. . . . A man-made mountain of stone built four thousand years ago . . . on a scale yet to be equalled. The sight of it sounds a chord in my heart, and I feel tears running down my cheeks. Nothing prepares you for the towering majesty of the last surviving wonder of the ancient world. It looks designed to outlast every work of man that ever was or will be. Instantly it is clear why so many for so long have felt it must mean something. . . . If, as Goethe [a German author] suggested, architecture is frozen music, then Egypt contains some of the greatest symphonies in the world.[62]

Reminders such as the Great Pyramid, however, left only picture images of Egypt's history. The hieroglyphics that decorated ancient walls and told the stories of the pharaohs were not at first recognized as a form of writing. Instead, archaeologists thought that the hieroglyphics served as religious or magical symbols. With no text to read, and no person to tell the story, many of ancient Egypt's accomplishments, as well as its legacy to today's world, remained a mystery.

Then, in 1799, a French soldier, part of an army that accompanied Napoleon to Egypt, was digging outside the town of Rosetta. Suddenly, he discovered a black basalt stone on which was carved three different forms of writing. The first two were Egyptian—hieroglyphics and demotic—and were unreadable to the discoverers. But the third kind of writing was Greek, which they recognized.

Using this Rosetta Stone, as it was called, Jean-Francois Champollion was able to use the Greek portion to decipher hieroglyphics in 1822. With the mystery solved, people now could read about the thoughts and deeds of the people of ancient Egypt. Scholars agree that more has been learned about ancient Egypt since Champollion deciphered hieroglyphics than at any other time within the past two thousand years. In fact, the entire science of Egyptology evolved as a result of it.

A Direct Legacy

Through trade and conquest, then, many ideas that originated in ancient Egypt were passed on to different cultures and different times. Products as varied as linen, glass, and even mosquito netting, invented by the Egyptians, found their way to points all over the world, and all are part of the legacy left by this ancient culture.

The Egyptians also left a great medical legacy, passing their knowledge on to other people through the first medical "textbooks" written on great papyrus scrolls. The science of medicine in ancient Egypt offered the world the idea of specialists. The Greeks seized upon it first: Herodotus observed that "each physician

In 1822 scholar Jean-Francois Champollion broke the code of Egyptian hieroglyphics by deciphering the writing on the Rosetta Stone (pictured).

applies himself to one disease only, and not more. Some physicians are for the eyes, others for the head, others for the teeth."[63] Egyptian surgical methods were later incorporated in the writings of Hippocrates, who is known as the founder of scientific medicine.

The sophistication of Egyptian drugs was known far and wide. The names of many of them occur in Hebrew, Syrian, and Persian medical works. The Greeks also copied Egyptian prescriptions, and they, too, appear in the writings of Hippocrates. Some of the drugs, such as opium and castor oil, developed during that millennia-old medical practice are still used today.

The Beauties of Karnak

The Temple of Karnak at Thebes ranks with the Great Pyramid as a glorious example of the skill of Egyptian architects. One of untold numbers of visitors to Karnak, Amelia B. Edwards describes her reaction in A Thousand Miles Up the Nile, *published in 1888.*

"How often has it been written, and how often must it be repeated, that the Great Hall of Karnak is the noblest architectural work ever designed and executed by human hands? One writer tells us that it covers four times the area occupied by the Cathedral of Notre Dame in Paris. Another measures it against St. Peter's. All admit their inability to describe it; yet all attempt the description. To convey a concrete image of the place to one who has not seen it, is, however, as I have already said, impossible. If it could be likened to this place or that, the task would not be so difficult; but there is, in truth, no building in the wide world to compare with it. The pyramids are more stupendous. The Colosseum [a huge outdoor theater in ancient Rome] covers more ground. The Parthenon [a temple in ancient Greece] is more beautiful. Yet [in] nobility of conception, in vastness of detail, in majesty of the highest order, the Hall of Pillars exceeds them every one. . . . You are stupefied [dumbfounded] by the thought of the mighty men who made them. You say to yourself: 'They were indeed giants in those days.'"

The Great Hall in the Temple of Karnak is an acclaimed architectural achievement.

The Egyptians, who developed the science of mathematics for use in monument building, laid the foundation for its development by other civilizations. Our counting system is based on theirs. Egyptian fractions were used by the Greeks, the Romans, and on into the Middle Ages, until modified into their current form. And many scholars believe the Egyptians' mathematical formulas to measure area and volume were passed to Greeks, who then fully developed geometry. Herodotus even wrote that geometry had an Egyptian origin.

The continuing influence of Egyptian architecture also is a direct legacy from Egypt. The Greeks, for example, are credited with the development of unique and graceful columns that adorn courthouses, museums, factories, railway stations, hotels, and churches throughout Europe and America. Some scholars, like James Henry Breasted, believe Greek architects were inspired by the temples of the Egyptian empire, with their graceful columns and pillared hypostyle halls.

Not only the Greeks, but the Romans and architects down through the centuries to the present day have been influenced by the Egyptians. One of the most famous examples in the United States is the Washington Monument in Washington, D.C., which has the shape of an Egyptian obelisk. More than five hundred feet high, it is the tallest monument of this kind in the world. Today, similar obelisks can be seen in London; Paris; Istanbul; and Rome, directly in front of the Vatican.

Egyptian art and architecture has had such an impact on our modern world that, as scholar Jean Capart says, "Egypt reveals

Some experts believe that Egyptian columns, such as these intricately carved columns in an Egyptian temple, inspired the graceful columns seen in Greek architecture.

Their Names Last for Many Lifetimes

Much of the great legacy of ancient Egypt was locked in the mystery of its writings until hieroglyphics were deciphered. But the Egyptians understood that the power of the written word can transcend the centuries, as is shown in this quote from George Steindorff and Keith C. Seele's, When Egypt Ruled the East.

"Though doors and houses were made for them [scribes], they are fallen to ruin. Their . . . tombstones are covered with earth, and their burial-chambers are forgotten. Their names, however, are [still] pronounced because of the books which they made, for they were good, and the memory of him who made them continues forever. Write, therefore—put that in your heart—and your name shall fare likewise. More beneficial is a book than carved stele [stone slab or pillar] or a solid tomb wall. . . . A man decays, his corpse is dust, and all his relatives are defunct [dead]; but the writings cause his name to be remembered in the mouth of the orator [speaker]. More beneficial is a book than the house of the builder or a mortuary chapel [funeral temple] in the west."

Egyptian hieroglyphics from a sixteenth-century B.C. book discovered in 1872. After hieroglyphics were deciphered, many of the mysteries of ancient Egypt were revealed.

to us the knowledge of one of the sources—perhaps the source—from which the great river of beauty has flowed continuously through the world."[64] And some of their skill still eludes us. In 1978, the Nippon Corporation of Japan, using the methods of the ancient Egyptians, tried to build a pyramid similar to the one at Giza. The attempt failed miserably, even after the workers brought in modern equipment.

An Indirect Legacy

Egyptian culture has also indirectly influenced Western society. Although today's Western calendar is not exactly like Egypt's ancient calendar, which has been called "the only intelligent calendar which ever existed in human history," there are many similarities.[65] Like the Egyptians', the calendar is based on the sun's movements rather than on those of the moon.

Another important part of the heritage from the Egyptians was the invention of papyrus. Although today's paper methods are inherited from the Chinese, papyrus, Egypt's early paper, provided us with an indirect legacy. Papyrus scrolls were exported to other parts of the ancient world, including Greece and Rome, where people used the scrolls to record their own literary works and other accounts. Thus, important knowledge that helped form the basis of our modern Western civilization was preserved and transmitted through the centuries. In fact, one author states, "If the Greek manuscripts [on Egyptian papyrus] had not been . . . preserved and been accessible, then few of the 16th century renaissance discoveries would have been possible."[66]

Egyptian literature, too, has made an impact on many peoples, including the Hebrews of Palestine. One area in which this can be seen is poetry. The Psalms, religious poems in the Old Testament of the Bible, are very similar to Egyptian poems written much earlier. For example, the words of Psalm 104 glorifying the Hebrew god, Yahweh, are very like Akhenaten's hymn praising the sun god, Aten. Psalm 104 declares, "In wisdom hast thou made them all; the earth is full of thy creatures."[67] The ancient Egyptian hymn says, "Thou didst create the earth according to thy desire. Men, all cattle large and small, all that are upon the earth."[68] Through this influence on the Old Testament, Egypt made an impact on Western literature.

The stories of the pharaohs and their times have continued to inspire us and spark our imaginations in movies, books, and poems. In his famous poem, "Ozymandias," Percy Bysshe Shelley describes a statue of Ramses II (who was sometimes called Ozymandias), thousands of years old, fallen and forgotten in the sand:

> I met a traveler from an antique land,
>
> Who said: Two vast and trunkless legs of stone
>
> Stand in the desert. Near them, on the sand,
>
> Half sunk, a shattered visage lies, whose frown,
>
> And wrinkled lip, and sneer of cold command,
>
> Tell that its sculptor well those passions read,
>
> Which yet survive, stamped on these lifeless things,

The legacy of Egypt's culture continues today, and new discoveries continue to intrigue the modern world. Here, a researcher peers into the entrance of the recently discovered family crypt of Ramses II.

The hand that mocked them, and the
  heart that fed:

And on the pedestal these words
  appear:

"My name is Ozymandias, King of
  Kings:

Look on my works, ye Mighty, and
  despair!"

Nothing beside remains. Round the
  decay

Of that colossal wreck, boundless and
  bare

The lone and level sands stretch far
  away. [69]

The legacy of Egypt's culture also influences our lives in subtle yet important ways. Tourists from around the world still travel to Egypt to see the remnants of its greatness. Fascination with this period drew thousands upon thousands of visitors when the treasures of Tutankhamen went on tour in the United States. This fascination was heightened by the recent discovery of Ramses II's great family crypt, which may contain the mummies of fifty-two of his sons, in the Valley of the Kings. People everywhere wait in eager anticipation for word of further discoveries.

Although millennia have passed since their civilization flourished, the world is deeply indebted to the ancient Egyptians. Whether their gifts to modern civilization were direct or indirect, they made their mark in many fields. As Herodotus explained when describing this perhaps never-equaled culture, "There is no country that possesses so many wonders, nor any which has such a number of works which defy description." [70]

Notes

Introduction: Ancient Clues

1. Quoted in Christopher Frayling, *The Face of Tutankhamun*. London: Faber and Faber, 1992.
2. Quoted in Frayling, *The Face of Tutankhamun*.

Chapter 1: The Roots of Egyptian Civilization

3. Quoted in National Geographic Society, *Ancient Egypt: Discovering Its Splendors*. Washington, DC: National Geographic Society, 1978.
4. Quoted in Christine Hobson, *Exploring the World of the Pharaohs*. London: Paul Press Ltd., 1987.
5. Adolf Erman, *Life in Ancient Egypt*. Translated by H. M. Tirard. New York: Dover Publications, 1971.
6. Quoted in Judith Crosher, *Ancient Egypt*. New York: Viking, 1992.
7. Quoted in T. G. H. James, *Pharaoh's People: Scenes from Life in Imperial Egypt*. Chicago: University of Chicago Press, 1984.

Chapter 2: The Old Kingdom: Egypt's Greatest Age

8. Quoted in George Steindorff and Keith C. Seele, *When Egypt Ruled the East*. Chicago: University of Chicago Press, 1957.
9. Quoted in Daniel Cohen, *Ancient Egypt*. New York: Doubleday, 1990.
10. *The Pyramid Texts*, ca. 2300 B.C., quoted in Paul William Roberts, *River in the Desert: Modern Travels in Ancient Egypt*. New York: Random House, 1993.
11. Quoted in Hobson, *Exploring the World of the Pharaohs*.
12. James Henry Breasted, *A History of Egypt: From the Earliest Times to the Persian Conquest*. New York: Charles Scribner's Sons, 1945.

13. Quoted in the Editors of Time-Life Books, *Egypt: Land of the Pharaohs*. Alexandria, VA: Time-Life Books, 1992.
14. Quoted in Roberts, *River in the Desert*.
15. Quoted in Leonard Cottrell, *Life Under the Pharaohs*. London: Pan Books, Ltd., 1955.
16. Quoted in S. R. K. Glanville, ed., *The Legacy of Ancient Egypt*. Oxford: Clarendon Press, 1942.

Chapter 3: Egyptian Society in Old Kingdom Memphis

17. Quoted in K. A. Kitchen, *Pharaoh Triumphant: The Life and Times of Rameses II, King of Egypt*. Warminster, England: Aris & Phillips, Ltd., 1982.
18. Breasted, *A History of Egypt*.
19. Quoted in Erman, *Life in Ancient Egypt*.
20. Quoted in Hobson, *Exploring the World of the Pharaohs*.
21. Erman, *Life in Ancient Egypt*.
22. Breasted, *A History of Egypt*.
23. Quoted in Cottrell, *Life Under the Pharaohs*.
24. Quoted in James, *Pharaoh's People*.
25. Quoted in Cottrell, *Life Under the Pharaohs*.
26. Quoted in Pierre Montet, *Everyday Life in Egypt in the Days of Rameses the Great*. Translated by A. R. Maxwell-Hyslop and Margaret S. Drower. Philadelphia: University of Pennsylvania Press, 1981.

Chapter 4: Chaos Reigns in Egypt

27. Quoted in Jaromir Malek, *In the Shadow of the Pyramids: Egypt During the Old Kingdom*. Norman: University of Oklahoma Press, 1986.
28. Quoted in Thomas W. Africa, *The Ancient World*. Boston: Houghton Mifflin, 1969.
29. Quoted in Breasted, *A History of Egypt*.

30. Quoted in Breasted, *A History of Egypt.*

31. Quoted in Breasted, *A History of Egypt.*

32. Quoted in Breasted, *A History of Egypt.*

33. Quoted in H. E. Winlock, *The Rise and Fall of the Middle Kingdom in Thebes.* New York: Macmillan, 1947.

Chapter 5: The Middle Kingdom: A New Egypt Arises

34. Quoted in Breasted, *A History of Egypt.*

35. Quoted in Africa, *The Ancient World.*

36. Quoted in Breasted, *A History of Egypt.*

37. Quoted in Breasted, *A History of Egypt.*

38. Quoted in Africa, *The Ancient World.*

39. Quoted in Breasted, *A History of Egypt.*

40. Quoted in Sir Alan Gardiner, *Egypt of the Pharaohs: An Introduction.* Oxford: Clarendon Press, 1961.

41. Quoted in Gardiner, *Egypt of the Pharaohs.*

Chapter 6: The New Kingdom: The Egyptian Empire

42. Quoted in Breasted, *A History of Egypt.*

43. Quoted in James Baikie, *A History of Egypt: From the Earliest Times to the End of the XVIIIth Dynasty.* Freeport, NY: Books for Libraries Press, 1971.

44. Quoted in Robert Silverberg, *Akhenaten: The Rebel Pharaoh.* New York: Chilton Books, 1964.

45. Quoted in Breasted, *A History of Egypt.*

46. Quoted in Philipp Vandenberg, *Nefertiti: An Archaeological Biography.* Philadelphia: J. B. Lippincott, 1978.

47. Quoted in Silverberg, *Akhenaten.*

48. Quoted in Silverberg, *Akhenaten.*

49. Quoted in Lichtheim, *Ancient Egyptian Literature,* in Nicholas Grimal, *A History of Ancient Egypt.* Translated by Ian Shaw. Oxford: Blackwell, Ltd., 1992.

50. Quoted in National Geographic Society, *Ancient Egypt.*

Chapter 7: The Decline of Ancient Egypt

51. Quoted in Breasted, *A History of Egypt.*

52. Quoted in Morris Brierbrier, *The Tomb-Builders of the Pharaohs.* London: British Museum Publications, 1982.

53. Quoted in Brierbrier, *The Tomb-Builders of the Pharaohs.*

54. Quoted in Gardiner, *Egypt of the Pharaohs.*

55. Quoted in Arthur Weigall, *The Glory of the Pharaohs.* London: Thornton Butterworth, Ltd., 1923.

56. Quoted in Weigall, *The Glory of the Pharaohs.*

57. Quoted in Grimal, *A History of Ancient Egypt.*

58. Quoted in Barbara Mertz, *Temples, Tombs, and Hieroglyphs: A Popular History of Ancient Egypt.* New York: Dodd, Mead, 1978.

59. Quoted in Gardiner, *Egypt of the Pharaohs.*

Chapter 8: The Legacy of the Ancient Egyptians

60. Quoted in Roberts, *River in the Desert.*

61. Quoted in Glanville, *The Legacy of Ancient Egypt.*

62. Roberts, *River in the Desert.*

63. Quoted in Janet Van Duyn, *The Egyptians: Pharaohs and Craftsmen.* New York: McGraw-Hill, n.d.

64. Quoted in Glanville, *The Legacy of Ancient Egypt.*

65. Quoted in J. R. Harris, ed., *The Legacy of Ancient Egypt.* Oxford: Clarendon Press, 1971.

66. Quoted in Anthony T. Browder, *Nile Valley Contributions to Civilization.* Washington, DC: The Institute of Karmic Guidance, 1992.

67. Quoted in Breasted, *A History of Egypt.*

68. Breasted, *A History of Egypt.*

69. Quoted in Louis Untermeyer, ed., *A Treasury of Great Poems.* New York: Simon & Schuster, 1962.

70. Quoted in Van Duyn, *The Egyptians.*

For Further Reading

Frances M. Clapham, *Ancient Civilizations.* New York: Warwick Press, 1978. Contains a fairly brief synopsis of ancient Egyptian civilization, which begins chronologically and shifts into a topical presentation.

Daniel Cohen, *Ancient Egypt.* New York: Doubleday, 1990. Beautifully illustrated, easy-to-read work that covers the history and civilization of ancient Egypt by topic.

Leonard Cottrell, *The Warrior Pharaohs.* New York: G. P. Putnam's Sons, 1969. A well-written work that deals exclusively with the warrior kings who made Egypt great from Menes to Ramses III. Uses extensive primary source quotations to help tell the story.

Judith Crosher, *Ancient Egypt.* New York: Viking, 1992. From the mysteries of the pyramids to the simplicity of a simple village home, the daily lives of the ancient Egyptians are revealed in a strong topical narrative and in stunning see-through cutaways.

Shirley Glubok and Alfred Tamarin, *The Mummy of Rahmose: The Life and Death of an Ancient Egyptian Nobleman.* New York: Harper & Row, 1978. Extremely well written story of Rahmose, vizier to Amenhotep III of the 18th Dynasty, encompassing the art, culture, religion, politics, and history of ancient Egypt at the height of its glory.

George Hart, *Exploring the Past: Ancient Egypt.* San Diego: Harcourt Brace Jovanovich, 1988. A comprehensive, topical presentation that describes the daily life of the ancient Egyptians. Beautifully illustrated, this book intends to give students a start in Egyptology.

Burnham Holmes, *Nefertiti: The Mystery Queen.* Milwaukee: Raintree Publishers, 1977. An extremely well written history of the life of Nefertiti, queen of ancient Egypt and Great Royal Wife of the rebel pharaoh Akhenaten.

Jill Kamil, *The Ancient Egyptians: How They Lived and Worked.* Chester Springs, PA: DuFour Additions, 1977. A look at how the ancient Egyptians of the Old Kingdom—Egypt's greatest age—lived and worked. The foundations of the Old Kingdom in Predynastic and Early Dynastic times are also included.

Vivian Koenig, *The Ancient Egyptians: Life in the Nile Valley.* Brookfield, CT: The Millbrook Press, 1992. Attractively illustrated topical overview of Egypt's history.

Fiona MacDonald, *Ancient Egyptians.* New York: Quarto Publishing, 1992. Fascinating tale of how ancient Egyptians lived and what they achieved. Packed with photographs, the book also features amazing foldout maps with illustrations that make life in ancient Egypt come alive.

Robin May, *Mysteries of the Pharaohs.* Chicago: Rand McNally, 1977. A very well written work with attractive illustrations that covers the life of a peasant boy named Nekhebu who served Ramses the Great. Through Nekhebu, the author topically covers many aspects of life in ancient Egypt.

Jacqueline Morley, Mark Bergin, and John James, *An Egyptian Pyramid.* New York: Peter Bedrick Books, 1991. Explores the Great Pyramid of Giza, which is representative of the ancient Egyptian culture, and depicts the life that evolved around it.

Elizabeth Payne, *The Pharaohs of Ancient Egypt.* New York: Random House, 1964. An extremely well written overview designed to interest students in the course of ancient Egyptian history. Uses a chronological approach that focuses on key individuals and important archaeological discoveries.

Nicholas Reeves, *Into the Mummy's Tomb: The Real-Life Discovery of Tutankhamun's Treasures.* Toronto, Ontario: Madison Press Books, 1992. Tells the gripping, true-life story of the discovery and exploration of Tutankhamen's tomb and all its treasures.

Miriam Schlein, *I, Tut: The Boy Who Became Pharaoh.* New York: Four Winds Press, 1979. Fascinating tale of Tutankhamen.

Robert Silverberg, *Akhenaten: The Rebel Pharaoh.* New York: Chilton Books, 1964. Adeptly uses primary sources to tell the story of Akhenaten, who, according to the author, was the greatest of all the pharaohs.

Carter Smith III, *The Pyramid Builders.* Morristown, NJ: Silver Burdett, 1991. An overview of Egyptian history that highlights the spirit of the pyramid builders and their extraordinary civilization, emphasizing the legacy they left future generations.

R. J. Unstead, *An Egyptian Town.* New York: Warwick Press, 1986. A colorfully illustrated story of Akhetaten, the pharaoh Akhenaten's great new capital city. In describing the city, the author paints a highly interesting picture of life in Egypt during the 18th Dynasty.

Philipp Vandenberg, *Nefertiti: An Archaeological Biography.* Philadelphia: J. B. Lippincott, 1978. Tears away the shrouds that have hidden the story of Egypt's fabled queen and reveals a life rich in excitement, intrigue, power, and tragedy.

Piero Ventura and Gian Paolo Ceserani, *In Search of Tutankhamun.* Morristown, NJ: Silver Burdett, 1985. Describes the discovery of Tutankhamen's tomb and gives a topical overview of life in Egypt.

Works Consulted

Thomas W. Africa, *The Ancient World.* Boston: Houghton Mifflin, 1969. A comphrehensive survey of the ancient world that includes a section on ancient Egypt.

James Baikie, *A History of Egypt: From the Earliest Times to the End of the XVIIIth Dynasty.* Freeport, NY: Books for Libraries Press, 1971. A detailed, comprehensive history of ancient Egypt by an early leader in the field of Egyptology.

John Baines and Jaromir Malek, *Atlas of Ancient Egypt.* New York: Facts On File, 1980. Presents Egyptian culture in the form of an atlas with a substantial narrative and many colorful illustrations. Along with focusing topically on life in ancient Egypt, the authors also take the reader on a trip down the Nile.

James Henry Breasted, *A History of Egypt: From the Earliest Times to the Persian Conquest.* New York: Charles Scribner's Sons, 1945. A clearly written survey of ancient Egyptian history; one of the first works of its kind and a standard in the field.

Morris Brierbrier, *The Tomb-Builders of the Pharaohs.* London: British Museum Publications, 1982. A reconstruction of the daily life of the workers who lived in the village of Deir el-Medina and labored on the tombs in the Valley of the Kings.

British Museum Publications, Ltd., *An Introduction to Ancient Egypt.* Oxford: British Museum Publications, Ltd., 1979. Provides an outline of the physical, historical, and cultural background of ancient Egypt.

Anthony T. Browder, *Nile Valley Contributions to Civilization.* Washington DC: The Institute of Karmic Guidance, 1992. Discusses in detail the contributions ancient Egyptians made to later civilizations, with a special emphasis on the African connection.

Leonard Cottrell, *Life Under the Pharaohs.* London: Pan Books, Ltd., 1955. Excellent, extremely readable book on the pharaohs' people and how they lived.

Adolf Erman, *Life in Ancient Egypt.* Translated by H. M. Tirard. New York: Dover Publications, 1971. Classic work, originally published in 1894, that covers the manners and customs, as well as the history, of ancient Egypt both chronologically and topically.

Christopher Frayling, *The Face of Tutankhamun.* London: Faber and Faber, 1992. Discusses the impact of the discovery of the tomb, rather than Tutankamen himself. Enhanced by quotations from the participants in the expedition, along with related short accounts of the time.

Sir Alan Gardiner, *Egypt of the Pharaohs: An Introduction.* Oxford: Clarendon Press, 1961. Fine introduction to Egyptian history aimed at luring readers into further study. Uses extensive primary sources, especially from Manetho.

S. R. K. Glanville, ed., *The Legacy of Ancient Egypt.* Oxford: Clarendon Press, 1942.

Details the heritage left to other civilizations by ancient Egyptians down to modern times.

Nicholas Grimal, *A History of Ancient Egypt.* Oxford: Blackwell, Ltd., 1992. A well-written, well-researched survey of Egyptian history with heavy reliance on primary sources and a perspective that incorporates the latest discoveries and points of view.

J. R. Harris, ed., *The Legacy of Ancient Egypt.* Oxford: Clarendon Press, 1971. Discusses the legacy of ancient Egypt to other civilizations up to the present.

Christine Hobson, *Exploring the World of the Pharaohs.* London: Paul Press, Ltd., 1987. A general handbook to ancient Egypt that provides information to tourists visiting the fascinating sites of the land of the pharaohs.

Michael A. Hoffman, *Egypt Before the Pharaohs: The Prehistoric Foundations of Egyptian Civilization.* Austin: University of Texas Press, 1979. A comprehensive review of Egyptian archaeology dealing with prehistoric and Predynastic times, which brings to life these eras.

Erik Hornung, *The Valley of the Kings: Horizon of Eternity.* New York: Timken Publishers, 1990. Discusses ancient Egypt's visions of the world beyond death as preserved in paintings on the walls and ceilings of the New Kingdom royal tombs in the Valley of the Kings.

T. G. H. James, *Pharaoh's People: Scenes from Life in Imperial Egypt.* Chicago: University of Chicago Press, 1984. Widens the perceptions of ancient Egypt by examining the daily working lives of ordinary Egyptians during the 18th Dynasty.

K. A. Kitchen, *Pharaoh Triumphant: The Life and Times of Rameses II, King of Egypt.* Warminster, England: Aris & Phillips, Ltd., 1982. Sketches the life of Ramses II and his remarkable family against the backdrop of the stirring events of the 19th Dynasty.

Jaromir Malek, *In the Shadow of the Pyramids: Egypt During the Old Kingdom.* Norman: University of Oklahoma Press, 1986. Contains many special insights into the daily lives of Old Kingdom Egyptians.

Barbara Mertz, *Temples, Tombs, and Hieroglyphs: A Popular History of Ancient Egypt.* New York: Dodd, Mead, 1978. An informal study of all things Egyptian rather than a history book, with a strong, interesting narrative that focuses on the people of Egypt.

Pierre Montet, *Everyday Life in Egypt in the Days of Rameses the Great.* Translated by A. R. Maxwell-Hyslop and Magaret S. Drower. Philadelphia: University of Pennsylvania Press, 1981. A classic study of daily life in ancient Egypt during the time of the Ramesside kings by one of the leaders of modern Egyptology.

National Geographic Society, *Ancient Egypt: Discovering Its Splendors.* Washington, DC: National Geographic Society, 1978. A topical history of ancient Egypt that presents its glories through well-written narrative and high-quality color photographs.

Paul William Roberts, *River in the Desert: Modern Travels in Ancient Egypt.* New York: Random House, 1993. A very interesting text, which combines experiences, histories, anecdotes, feelings, and conversations, and is designed to make readers want to visit Egypt.

John Romer, *Ancient Lives: The Story of the Pharaohs' Tombmakers*. London: Weidenfeld & Nicolson, 1984. The biography of a three-thousand-year-old village, which tries to bring the ancient villagers to life and tells how national events affected their lives.

George Steindorff and Keith C. Seele, *When Egypt Ruled the East*. Chicago: University of Chicago Press, 1957. An absorbing introduction to Egyptian history, focusing chronologically on the golden age of empire.

Eugene Strouhal, *Life of the Ancient Egyptians*. Norman: University of Oklahoma Press, 1992. Lavishly illustrated book that conveys the wonders of ancient Egypt through a topical discussion of the daily activities of ordinary people.

The Editors of Time-Life Books, *The Age of God-Kings*. Alexandria, VA: Time-Life Books, 1987. A brief overview of Egyptian history and civilization.

The Editors of Time-Life Books, *Egypt: Land of the Pharaohs*. Alexandria, VA: Time-Life Books, 1992. A topical history of Egypt, beautifully illustrated and well written.

Janet Van Duyn, *The Egyptians: Pharaohs and Craftsmen*. New York: McGraw-Hill, n.d. Very well-written text that surveys the history of Egypt and makes it come alive for readers.

Arthur Weigall, *The Glory of the Pharaohs*. London: Thornton Butterworth, Ltd., 1923. A series of highly interesting essays on ancient Egypt by one of the early experts in the field of Egyptology, who has the talent to make readers see the past.

Evelyn Wells, *Nefertiti*. Garden City, NY: Doubleday, 1964. Through a highly interesting biography of Nefertiti, the readers learn about life during the 18th Dynasty and under the pharaoh Akhenaten.

Jon Manchip White, *Everyday Life in Ancient Egypt*. New York: Peter Bedrick Books, 1963. Discusses the daily life of ancient Egyptians throughout Dynastic times, portraying vividly everyone from the pharaoh to the nobles to the peasants.

H. E. Winlock, *The Rise and Fall of the Middle Kingdom in Thebes*. New York: Macmillan, 1947. A detailed, scholarly discussion of the Middle Kingdom.

Index

Picture Credits

Cover photo: © Brian Brake/Photo Researchers, Inc.

AKG, London, 34, 44, 72, 75, 76, 78, 80 (bottom), 81

Alinari/Art Resource, NY, 83

Archive Photos, 38, 64

The Bettmann Archive, 19, 30, 31, 41, 47, 53, 92, 97, 99

Bridgeman/Art Resource, NY, 94

The British Museum, 29

Foto Marburg/Art Resource, NY, 26, 27, 33, 67, 71, 74

Giraudon/Art Resource, NY, 22, 56, 87

Griffith Institute, Ashmolean Museum, Oxford, 12, 13, 79

Image Select, 80 (top)

Erich Lessing/Art Resource, NY, 46, 49, 65, 88

The Metropolitan Museum of Art, 18

North Wind Picture Archives, 84, 90

Photography by Egyptian Expedition, The Metropolitan Museum of Art, 28

Scala/Art Resource, NY, 61

Stock Montage, Inc., 20, 43, 54

Werner Forman Archive/The British Museum/Art Resource, NY, 40

Werner Forman Archive/The Egyptian Museum, Berlin/Art Resource, NY, 51

About the Author

Brenda Smith is an author and editor, specializing in elementary and secondary social studies education. During the past sixteen years, she has contributed to a variety of social studies textbooks and ancillary programs, many as an editor for the Merrill Publishing Company. Smith was selected as a delegate to the first United States–Russia Joint Conference on Education in Moscow in October 1994. She is also listed in *Who's Who in American Education* (1994–95), *Who's Who in the World* (1995–96), *Who's Who in American Women* (1995–96), *Dictionary of International Biography* (1995), and *Something about the Author* (1995). After receiving her bachelor's degree in history and government from Ohio University in Athens, Smith completed graduate course work there in American and European history. A former teacher, Smith is a member of the National Council for the Social Studies, the Ohio Council for the Social Studies, the Association for Supervision and Curriculum Development, and the Freelance Editorial Association.

DATE DUE
